RUNNING
INTO
NO MAN'S
LAND

The wisdom of
Woodbine Willie

CWR

ACKNOWLEDGEMENTS

With grateful thanks to: Lynette, for giving me the opportunity to write about a man whose life and work have inspired me over many years; Lauren, Ben and all the team at CWR, for excellence throughout; the Studdert Kennedy family, for permission to quote extensively from Woodbine Willie's writings; Ed, Luke, Rich, Samuel and Stuart for your erudite comments on the more theological/philosophical parts of the manuscript; the Council of the Oxford Pastorate, for allowing me time to work on this project; and, above all, my wonderful family, who ceaselessly inspire, support and encourage.

Copyright © Jonathan Brant 2014

Published 2014 by CWR, Waverley Abbey House, Waverley Lane, Farnham, Surrey GU9 8EP, UK. Registered Charity No. 294387. Registered Limited Company No. 1990308.

The right of Jonathan Brant to be identified as the author of this work has been asserted by him in accordance with the Copyright, Designs and Patents Act 1988, sections 77 and 78.

For a list of National Distributors visit www.cwr.org.uk/distributors

Unless otherwise indicated all Scripture references are from The Holy Bible, New International Version, (Anglicised edition), copyright © 1979, 1984, 2011 by Biblica (formerly International Bible society).

Other Scripture quotations are marked: ESV: The Holy Bible, English Standard Version copyright © 2001 by Crossway Bibles, a division of Good News Publishers. Used by permission. All rights reserved.

Concept development, editing, design and production by CWR.

Printed in the UK by Linney Group.

ISBN: 978-1-78259-265-5

CONTENTS:

INTRODUCTION

RUNNING INTO NO MAN'S LAND

It was a common enough scene in those days, an advanced collecting post for wounded in the Ypres Salient, on the evening of June 15th, 1917. Twenty men all smashed up and crammed together in a little concrete shelter which would have been full with ten in it. Outside the German barrage banging down all round us. The one guttering candle on the edge of a broken wire-bed going out every five minutes when a salvo of 5.9's from Pilkom Ridge shook the place to its foundations. A boy with a badly shattered thigh in a corner moaning and yelling by turns for "Somefing to stop the pain." So it had been for an hour or more. Between this Black Hole of Calcutta and Battalion H.Q. Death and Hell to go through. Hell inside and hell out, and the moaning of the boy in the corner like the moaning of a damned soul ...

There was no morphia. That was the horror. Some one must go for it. I went.[1]

The man who 'went' – running into no man's land, sheltering in shell holes, then running again – was Geoffrey Anketell Studdert Kennedy, better known as 'Woodbine Willie'. He was not a soldier but a chaplain whose unusual bravery won him the Military Cross. An official announcement explained: 'He showed the greatest courage and disregard for his own safety in attending to the wounded under heavy fire. He searched shell holes for our own, and enemy wounded, assisting them to the Dressing Station, and his cheerfulness and endurance had a splendid effect upon all the ranks in the front line trenches, which he constantly visited.'[2]

Woodbine Willie was also spiritually courageous. After the war he continued with a life dedicated to serving the suffering. Working as a travelling evangelist, he shivered and wheezed on freezing street corners, preaching hope into the hearts of labourers in dole queues. As a pastor in impoverished parishes, he railed against injustice and wept with couples whose marriages had descended into bitter cycles of betrayal and recrimination. And, ceaselessly, he wrestled with God, exploring fresh answers to life's toughest questions in his preaching and writing.

In the pages that follow, I would like to introduce you to some of the wisdom of Woodbine Willie as I have encountered it in his prose and his poetry. I believe that his wisdom, forged in the heat of battle and in loving service of the suffering, has power to speak into our lives, particularly where we struggle with doubt, confusion and disappointment.

Woodbine Willie wrought wisdom for every day of the week, not just for Sundays, and wisdom for all of life, not just the good times.

HOW TO READ THIS BOOK

This book is an introduction to Woodbine Willie's life and thought. It is not a systematic theology (for which, you are probably grateful), nor is it a comprehensive account of Christian life; rather it reflects Woodbine Willie's preoccupations and interests as it addresses a number of important aspects of the journey of faith.

There will not be time or space to address any issue in its fullness, but I hope this book will provide you with an opportunity to consider the Christian life from a fresh perspective, the perspective of this singular and fascinating figure, Woodbine Willie, and in the light of Scripture, to reflect and apply something of his wisdom to your walk with God.

Part 1 offers a first opportunity to get to know Woodbine Willie. A general introduction is followed by sketches of his life, his thought and his understanding of the shape of the Christian life. Parts 2-4 explore the wisdom of Woodbine Willie in greater detail, considering what he can teach us about living for God today. Each chapter in these parts will have the same format:

1. Introduction: To set the scene and present the topic to be considered
2. Woodbine Willie in his own words: An extended quotation from one of Woodbine Willie's many published writings
3. Discussion: Drawing out and highlighting the key argument or intent of the text
4. Reflection: Scripture readings, questions and prayers to help us reflect on Woodbine Willie's wisdom

Throughout this book, I will try to act as your guide. I believe a guide is necessary because Woodbine Willie lived his Christian life in a tradition that is perhaps unfamiliar to many of us. He was a committed High Church, sacramental Anglican. His discipleship was focused on the offices of morning and evening prayer and, especially, on the sacrament of communion which he took almost every day.

Furthermore, he considered himself a 'modernist' in his theology. He took for granted the findings of modern science and modern philosophy, including the historical critical method of reading the Bible, which more conservative Christians took to be attacks on the integrity of the Christian faith.

In addition, time has not stood still. History has moved on and the third millennium world we live in is very different to the world Woodbine Willie inhabited. Many of his references and many of the events he describes will be alien to us. He never used inclusive language and his persistent reference to 'men' and 'sons' might understandably alienate some contemporary readers. Sometimes we will need to think our way back into the shoes of those he originally wrote for, in order to understand the weight of what he is saying.

Ultimately, I'm a fan of Woodbine Willie and thank God for all he has to teach us, but there are places where I think we can best learn from him by disagreeing. After all, he was not afraid to change his mind when experience or study convinced him his earlier positions (eg his initial support of the war) were wrong. However, I hope at all times to be respectful of this remarkable servant of God, recognising that no-one this side of heaven has the whole truth, least of all me.

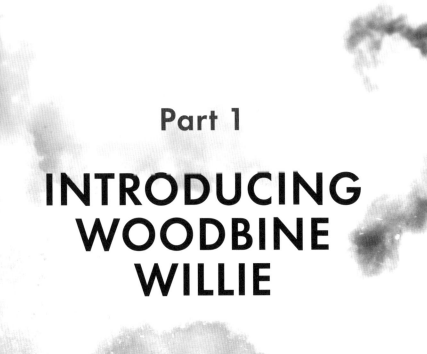

Part 1

INTRODUCING WOODBINE WILLIE

CHAPTER 1

WHY WOODBINE WILLIE?

My first encounter with Woodbine Willie came unexpectedly. I was in my early twenties, a graduate of Bible College, working in a café in central London while I tried to figure out what God would have me do with my life. My circle of Christian friends reflected the diversity of young adults in any large city-centre church, students, early-career professionals, casual workers like me, and, as it happened, a number of nurses.

It was our habit, after Sunday evening services, to walk around the corner to one of the nurses' residences for tea and cake and chat. One evening, as we sat waiting for the kettle to boil, someone pulled out a battered paperback and, without invitation or introduction, began to read (in a very dodgy cockney accent):

WELL?

Our Padre were a solemn bloke,
We called 'im dismal Jim.
It fairly gave ye t' bloomin' creeps,
To sit and 'ark at 'im,
When 'e were on wi' Judgement Day,
Abaht that great white throne,
And 'ow each chap would 'ave to stand,
And answer on 'is own.

I didn't know it at the time but I was hearing a 'dialect poem' written by Woodbine Willie. In these poems he tried to translate Christian doctrine into the language and the life experience of the working-class soldiers he served and loved.

This poem, which explores ideas of sin, judgment and repentance, continues with the narrator telling how he fell asleep and dreamt he was dead. But instead of a great white throne and a judgment court, he finds himself standing alone with his thoughts on the shore of a vast, placid sea:

And day by day, and year by year,
My life came back to me.
I seed just what I were, and what
I'd 'ad the charnce to be.
And all the good I might 'a' done,
And 'adn't stopped to do.
I seed I'd made an 'ash of it,
And Gawd! but it were true.
A throng o' faces came and went,
Afore me on that shore,
My wife, and mother, kiddies, pals,

11

> And the face of a London whore.
> And some was sweet, and some was sad,
> And some put me to shame,
> For the dirty things I'd done to 'em,
> When I 'adn't played the game.

The stream of reminiscence is only broken when the narrator becomes aware of a powerful presence standing before him:

> It seemed to me as though 'Is face
> Were millions rolled in one;
> It never changed yet always changed,
> Like the sea beneath the sun.
> 'Twere all men's face yet no man's face,
> And a face no man can see,
> And it seemed to say in silent speech,
> "Ye did 'em all to Me.
> The dirty things ye did to 'em,
> The filth ye thought was fine,
> Ye did 'em all to Me," it said,
> "For all their souls were Mine."
> All eyes was in 'Is eyes – all eyes,
> My wife's and a million more;
> And once I thought as those two eyes
> Were the eyes of the London whore.
> And they was sad – my Gawd, 'ow sad,
> Wiv tears what seemed to shine,
> And quivering bright wi' the speech o' light
> They said, "'Er soul was Mine."
> And then at last 'E said one word,
> 'E just said one word – "Well?"
> And I said in a funny voice,

> *"Please can I go to 'Ell?"*
> *And 'E stood there and looked at me,*
> *And 'E kind 'o seemed to grow,*
> *Till 'E shone like the sun above my 'ead,*
> *And then 'E answered "No,*
> *You can't, that 'Ell is for the blind,*
> *And not for those that see.*
> *You know that you 'ave earned it, lad,*
> *So you must follow Me."*
>
> *...*
>
> *There ain't no throne, and there ain't no books,*
> *It's 'Im you've got to see,*
> *It's 'Im, just 'Im, that is the Judge*
> *Of blokes like you and me.*
> *And, boys, I'd sooner frizzle up,*
> *I' the flames of a burnin' 'Ell,*
> *Than stand and look into 'Is face,*
> *And 'ear 'Is voice say – "Well?"[1]*

In the nurses' residence, the kettle whistled and the spell was broken. Insults and cushions were thrown in the speaker's direction. No one had requested a poetry recital, after all. But the poem stayed with me.

Days later I found myself in my Vicar's study and, as he was the only literary-type I knew, I described the poem and asked if he knew anything about it. He said he couldn't be sure (I'd no doubt mangled it beyond recognition) but it sounded like the work of the World War One chaplain Studdert Kennedy, commonly known as Woodbine Willie. I thanked him and promptly forgot about it.

Well, almost forgot. The unusually earthy language and the powerful images were lodged in my mind, now linked to the strange name of 'Woodbine Willie'. Years later, in a charity bookshop, an unusual title caught my eye – *The Unutterable Beauty*. I pulled the slim, hardback volume down off the shelf and inside I found the half-remembered poem and many others like it. My library of Woodbine Willie books was begun! And now, some twenty years later, I have that slim volume beside me, opened to the first poem I ever heard, and I have the privilege of introducing a few more people to the life and thought of this highly unusual Christian teacher.

In this introductory chapter I want to answer some questions. Actually, I want to answer the same question – Why Woodbine Willie? – three times. I want to explain: why Woodbine Willie has such a strange name, why Woodbine Willie is worthy of our attention, and why Woodbine Willie's wisdom might help us.

WHY 'WOODBINE WILLIE'?

BECAUSE THAT'S WHAT THE MEN HE LOVED NAMED HIM

As a chaplain, Woodbine Willie held officer rank and could have claimed the benefits, including relatively comfortable accommodations far from the frontlines. But he loved the men he served and chose to stay close to them. Writing of his practice of trying to cheer up the soldiers while they were under fire in the trenches, he explained his methods: 'I whispered some inane remark as I passed by, and was rewarded all along the line with a grin which even darkness could not hide, and often, when I had passed, with the muttered comment, "Gaw blyme if it ain't the parson"!'[2]

When in camp, he insisted on taking part in the physical training, even the hand-to-hand combat practice. He genuinely enjoyed the exercise and the company but also saw it as part of his mission. He wryly observed: 'After a man has had the exquisite pleasure of punching a parson's nose, he is the more ready to listen to him preach.'[3] His love for the soldiers coupled with his highly developed sense of humour and his extremely unusual ministry style explain why the men would give him an affectionate nickname. But why did they call him 'Woodbine Willie'?

A talk which Woodbine Willie gave in his parish while on home leave described an average day near the front and draws attention to the practice which earned the nickname. The talk was reported in the local press:

At 7:30 he said matins in a little chapel in an old barn, and if he could get any communicants he celebrated [communion] as well. Then he wrote letters till 10 o'clock and, after that, spent every day (except Sundays) from 11 to 6:30 in the lines. He took up a large box of Woodbines and some New Testaments, and marched round, sometimes talking about religion, and sometimes talking utter nonsense and playing the fool, but always giving away fags ... "I always go up with the men to a raid and that has tightened the bond between them and me enormously ... You must acquire the love of the men; be their comrade and friend."[4]

The comradeship, the humour and, of course, the Woodbine cigarettes, led the men to re-christen the unusual parson 'Woodbine Willie':

WOODBINE WILLIE

They gave me this name like their nature,
Compacted of laughter and tears,
A sweet that was born of the bitter,
A joke that was torn from the years.

Of their travail and torture, Christ's fools,
Atoning my sins with their blood,
Who grinned in their agony sharing
The glorious madness of God.

> *Their name! Let me hear it – the symbol*
> *Of unpaid – unpayable debt,*
> *For the men to whom I owed God's Peace,*
> *I put off with a cigarette.*[5]

WHY WOODBINE WILLIE?

BECAUSE HE WROUGHT GREAT WISDOM FROM GREAT SUFFERING

It is easy to think of the men and women who endured the First World War as a different breed. But up until 1916, when he was in his early thirties, Woodbine Willie had no more experience of war than most of us. Unsurprisingly, his sudden immersion into the horrors of trench warfare impacted him deeply. A few years later, he described what it was like to be, for the first time, in the midst of battle:

Battles were just the movements on the chess-board of the world to me. I was as innocent, as fatuously, idiotically innocent as most young men of my generation. I carried the interesting facts into my first battle, and there they came to life, they roared and thundered, they dripped with blood, they cursed, mocked, blasphemed, and cried like a child for mercy. They stood up before me like obscene spectres, beckoning with bloody hands, laughing like fiends at my little parochial religion, and my silly parochial God. I can remember running over an open space under shell-fire ... and every shrieking shell kept yelling at me with foul oaths: Now do you understand, you miserable little parson with your petty shibboleths, this is W-A-R-War, and History is War – and this is what History means. How about gentle Jesus, God the Father, and the

Peace of God – how about it? I saw the face of Christ in his agony, and remembered some Sunday School children singing in shrill, childish voices:

Peace on earth and mercy mild,
God and sinners reconciled

Then I found the man I was looking for, and stopped thinking.[6]

Woodbine Willie only stopped thinking for a moment, soon his sharp mind was questing again. Ceaselessly, restlessly he searched for answers to the mocking questions of the obscene spectres that delighted in war. It is the way in which he wrestled with such questions that makes him worthy of our attention now. He wanted to know:

Was God down in the Flanders mud or up in His heaven, safe on the far side of a sky black with artillery shells? Was God found in the slums among the ragged and the despairing, or only in the chapels of the wealthy and self-satisfied? Was God really the source of a hope more powerful than the horrors of war and the disappointments of peace? Was God truly offering the possibility of a radically new quality of life here and now, and the certainty of ultimate victory in the future, of this broken world remade and every tear wiped from every eye?

There was no guarantee that Woodbine Willie would find helpful answers to those questions. Our own experience tells us that suffering, or watching others suffer, does not automatically result in wisdom. Suffering can just as easily twist our thinking and lead to self-pity or incoherent rage. For every Nelson Mandela emerging from prison with a new perspective and a message of forgiveness, there are thousands driven by their suffering into hatred, bitterness and despair. But when wisdom does grow out of the stony ground of exceptionally harsh experience, it is a jewel 'more precious than rubies' (Prov. 8:11). We can learn a great deal from those few who have travelled through extreme suffering to return with uncommon wisdom. Woodbine Willie is worthy of our attention because he was such a man.

WHY WOODBINE WILLIE?

BECAUSE HE TURNED HARD THINKING INTO EASY READING

Woodbine Willie loved the ordinary people of Britain: the poor he served in parish life, the illiterate soldiers for whom he wrote letters home, the labouring men and women who would never willingly darken the door of a church or read a book of theology. He realised that it was not enough to wrestle with the complex challenges to Christian faith that were raised by the horrors of war. Any answers he found would have to be translated into a form that would be comprehensible to these ordinary people. It has been said, 'Simplicity on the nearside of complexity is worthless but simplicity on the far side of complexity is priceless.'[7] At their best, Woodbine Willie's writings have the stamp of priceless simplicity. He could use the language and the life-experience of the man and woman on the street to communicate ideas of great subtlety.

He was sometimes criticised for his down-to-earth approach but he responded bluntly: 'I write exactly as I think, and for the life of me cannot do otherwise. It is not good English and I am often painfully conscious of that fact, for I love good prose as I love fine poetry. But it takes more than style to redeem a man's soul.'[8] The principal reason for the lack of style was a lack of time. As we will see in the next chapter, Woodbine Willie worked himself into the ground. In a heartrendingly poignant introduction to one of his last books, he wrote:

The book I fear is as full of characteristic faults and failures as every other I have written. I wish it were better done. I still dream of a day when with ample leisure at my command, and a full and adequate preparation I shall be able to write down plainly what God means to me. But perhaps that is only a dream.[9]

Six months after he wrote those words Woodbine Willie died, never having found the time and leisure he so desired. Nonetheless, he left behind him a valuable body of work. His books may not have been polished or conventionally stylish but they were, and they remain, powerful. His thought still has the potential to benefit our walk with God.

CHAPTER 2

THE LIFE OF WOODBINE WILLIE

Woodbine Willie did not live long but he certainly lived life to the full. Biographies published about him are packed with incident and anecdote, for which I will not find space in this chapter. In view of the brevity of this account, I'll list some excellent resources at the end of this book, for those who would like to read more about the life and work of this fascinating man of faith.

EARLY LIFE AND MINISTRY

Geoffrey Anketell Studdert Kennedy (later to be known as Woodbine Willie) was born in Leeds on 27 June 1883.

His first home was in a deprived part of the city surrounded by rows of slum tenements, a large workhouse, and a pub cheerily named the 'Cemetery Tavern'.[1] The house was a vicarage and he came from a line of many generations of clergymen. His father, the Revd William Studdert Kennedy, was an Irishman who had come to England as a parish priest with a vocation to serve the poorest in society. He had five children with his first wife and a further six by his second even before Geoffrey's birth, after which there were still another two to come!

As might be imagined with so many children, the Kennedy home was always filled with noise. But, more importantly, it was filled with love. It's hard to be sure how much his later fame affected his family's memories of him but their recollections suggest that Geoffrey was a particularly good-natured child and full of fun. Even his struggles with asthma could not bring him down. He was also intellectually curious, easily absorbed into reading, conversation or games and, hence, sometimes distracted and forgetful.

A favourite family anecdote about Geoffrey's absentmindedness relates to what would appear a simple errand. Sent to the local greengrocer to order replenishments for the large family's larder, he walked into the shop deep in thought and as a result, something went amiss. When the requested delivery arrived later in the day, his frugal mother was horrified to receive two stones of strawberries and two pounds of potatoes in place of two pounds of strawberries and two stones of potatoes![2]

Even without grocery mix-ups courtesy of Geoffrey's absentmindedness, a large family living off a small clergy stipend left very little to spare even for highly valued goods and services. Therefore, most of Geoffrey's early education was an informal, family affair. Occasionally his mother taught him but more often his lessons were administered at the hands of elder brothers and sisters.

Fortunately, he was voracious in self-directed reading and thinking, often surprising older family members with strongly held positions on assorted issues of little immediate relevance to a young boy. From age nine he spent some time at a small private school and at age fourteen he won a place at Leeds Grammar School.

The unusual mix of exuberant individuality and careful thought that was to characterise his life and ministry was already coming to the fore. Commenting on his career at the grammar school, his lifelong friend J.K. Mozley wrote: 'To his school contemporaries he was always probably a bit of a wild Irishman but I think that those of us who knew him best realised something of the intellectual ability which lay behind his oddities. And from quite an early stage in my friendship with him I was struck with the fineness of his character.'[3]

His Irish roots made Trinity College, Dublin a natural choice of university. Following in his father's and his older brothers' footsteps, he applied and passed the entrance exams at the remarkably young age of fourteen. However, financial constraints prevented him from taking up his place until much later. Even when he was finally enrolled, lack of money meant he studied as an external student, spending very little time actually resident in Dublin. Undaunted by distance from lectures and tutors, he obtained a first class degree in classics and divinity and even won a medal for his academic achievements.[4]

After completing his studies at Trinity College, Geoffrey taught at Calday Grange Grammar School in the seaside town of West Kirby on the Wirral Peninsula. He appears to have been happy there in his teaching. He also threw himself into the wider life of the school and was particularly passionate about sports. Inevitably, he was wildly popular with the pupils.[5]

In spite of his contentment in the life of a teacher, he was contemplating a different calling. While there was no blinding flash of light or booming voice from heaven, his personal faith, family heritage and a vocation to serve the poor eventually led him to offer himself to the Church of England for ordination.

He trained at Ripon Clergy College in Yorkshire before being ordained in Worcester Cathedral in 1908 and sent to work in Rugby. In Rugby, his ministry focused on the same parts of society his father had served. He directed his remarkable energies towards those most in need. A colleague during those early years later became Bishop of Blackburn. He never forgot Geoffrey's unique approach:

For him the setting and the stage of religion was this world, and his own intense humanness kept his intellectual side harnessed, if not subordinate to his pastoral work. I can see again that small slim figure strolling into the unattractive Public House where his beloved lodging-house tramps were to be found and standing up in the bar in his cassock to sing 'Nazareth', while half his audience 'felt within a power unfelt before'. They loved him – loved him for his great laugh, the smile that transformed his face, the inimitable Irish brogue, but most of all because of his love for them.[6]

Indeed, Woodbine Willie's love for the poor was such that throughout his life he frequently found himself in financial trouble. His generosity sometimes led him into damaging personal debt and, later in life, into conflict with his longsuffering wife. For example, she was less than pleased when he gave away their bed, carrying it piece-by-piece down the street to an old woman in need of comfortable rest.[7]

In money matters he was hopeless – no half-crown found it possible to stay in his pocket for more than a few hours. His friends rejoiced when his excellent housekeeper insisted on his handing all his money over to her, but even she could not prevent him giving away his clothes ... he could not help giving: his heart was as big as his mind and like his mind was always overflowing.[8]

Geoffrey's mother died the year he was ordained. So, after four years of curacy in Rugby, he returned to Leeds to support his father who, in spite of his advanced age, continued his parish ministry to the urban poor.

While his principal role continued to be pastoral care of the disadvantaged, Geoffrey also began to develop a taste for open-air preaching. His love of engaging those who would never have entered a church, and crossing swords verbally with spirited hecklers, stood him in good stead later in his ministry when he preached to large companies of terrified soldiers and to great crowds of disillusioned workers.

Throughout his ministry in Leeds, Geoffrey continued to practise sports. It was through a football team that he met a young trainee solicitor who was reckless enough to introduce the wild young cleric to his pretty sister. The sister's name was Emily Catlow and Woodbine Willie fell in love with her, marrying her on 25 April 1914. He remained devoted to Emily for the rest of his life. He was ever grateful to God for her selfless support of him through the challenges of war and, after the war, an increasingly itinerant ministry.

Later that year, Geoffrey's father died aged 88 and he felt free to seek another parish. But, typically, he turned down invitations from comfortable suburbs where large churches wanted him for his vibrant preaching and sensitive pastoral care. Instead, waiting only to receive assurance from his bride that she was willing to live on a low stipend in an impoverished district, he took the very poor parish of St Paul's, Worcester.[9]

WAR YEARS

Shortly after Geoffrey and Emily were married, Britain went to war with Germany. Geoffrey supported the government in its decision to declare war, agreed with the allies' war aims, and actively encouraged the young men of Worcester to volunteer for the army. But he did not immediately enlist. There was no cowardice or hypocrisy in this decision; he was committed to his parish ministry among the needy and, like many others, did not expect a long conflict. It was in 1915 that he took the decision to go to France to minister to the British forces now unexpectedly mired in a bloody war of attrition.

Soon after his arrival in France he wrote an open letter home to his parish describing the first communion service he conducted, on Christmas Day 1915. It was published in *Berrow's Worcester Journal*:

My Dear People

The first place where we were sent was a little French village which in summer, and in happier times, must be a beautiful place, but it was desolate that Christmas morning ... I found 400 men drawn up in the rain, waiting patiently. It would have made your heart glad and sad at once to see the men ... I was glad and very thankful to God for bringing me there. We had a short service and a sermon which preached itself. Then the glorious part came. I went into a shed in the farmyard and the communicants came to me. There were not many, but they meant it. It was wonderful, no lights, no ritual, nothing to help but the rain and the far off roll of guns, and Christ was born in a cattle shed on Christmas Day. He came silently and surely nearer – nearer to us, officers and men kneeling on the mud floor, and we all knew it. I thanked God for sending me, and you for letting me go ...

I must draw to a close now. I shall go up to the Front in my time.

Yours ever in Christ

The Vicar[10]

Geoffrey's unique ministry style as a chaplain was simply a variation of the approach he had long used among the urban poor. His desire to be with the people remained the same. He no longer met them in dirty pubs and boarding houses but in cavernous railway sheds, rowdy mess tents and, of course, the trenches. He still gave impromptu singing performances, adjusting his sometimes comic, sometimes sentimental repertoire and choosing songs to touch the hearts of the sons, husbands and lovers among the men. He would then serve the often illiterate soldiers by writing letters home to their mothers, wives and girlfriends.

As the men boarded trains, or formed into long snaking columns for the journey to the frontlines and into battle, he would walk up and down with a large canvas sack. From within he would pull New Testaments and packets of Woodbines cigarettes. Captain Geoffrey Studdert Kennedy was soon forgotten and Woodbine Willie was born.

> *'Has Captain Kennedy gone along?' an officer looking for Geoffrey once asked of a sentry. 'No, sir.'*
> *'Have you seen the Chaplain, then?'*
> *'No, sir.'*
> *'Have you had the padre this way?'*
> *'No, sir.'*
> *'Look,' said the officer, 'have you seen Woodbine Willie lately?'*
> *'Yes, sir: just gone by.'*[11]

Woodbine Willie later observed that while it was obvious what the soldiers wanted with the cigarettes, it was impossible to know why they took the Bibles. Was it desire for the truth they contained, sentiment, or just superstition? 'Yes, I'll 'ave one, sir; you never know your luck; it may stop a bullet,' was a remark he remembered hearing more than once.[12]

Woodbine Willie's first experience of the frontlines was in one of the most infamous battles of the whole war, the Battle of the Somme, which raged from the heat of summer into the slushy snow of autumn 1916. With over a million men killed, it was a hellish baptism of fire for a new chaplain. In his biography of Woodbine Willie, Bob Holman offers this summary of his duties through this period:

> He ensured that he was always present when the men prepared to go over the top. Inevitably, he distributed Woodbines. When the whistle blew for the advance, he was in the midst. Once over the top, the men usually faced bullets and shells, with many mown down. He then sought out the wounded and the dying. The former he often dragged out of the mud, got onto a stretcher, and pulled to the first aid post, ducking shells as they went. Sometimes he dragged the stretchers through flooded trenches. At times, he lay on his belly as he attempted to comfort the dying. After the fighting ceased, he returned to the makeshift hospital to remain with the badly wounded or to hold a man down as the doctor operated on him without anaesthetic. Often, he went twenty-four hours without sleep and with little food. At times, he spluttered and coughed with his asthma. After the fighting, he gathered a few volunteers, and buried as many of the dead as could be found.[13]

The reference to Woodbine Willie's asthma is poignant as the conditions in the trenches and the exertions of his ministry seem to have worsened the respiratory problems that had troubled him since childhood. There were periods of severe illness requiring hospitalisation in France and short periods of leave back in England.

However, it was not his physical limitations but his gifting which led to his being taken from the frontlines and assigned to other duties for parts of the war. As one of the few preachers with the ability to command the attention of boisterous troops gathered in the open air, he was assigned by the Chaplain General to a wandering role, speaking in many different camps, bases and staging posts along the Western Front.

The priest who refused to go to comfortable parishes was equally unwilling to be pulled back from the front lines. He initially refused the order and requested to be sent back to the trenches but his superiors persisted and, eventually, he complied. Thus began a period of ministry that was less dangerous but not less exhausting. He preached up to three times every day of the week, often in the open air, and to crowds of between 500 and 1,500 soldiers.

At one point he was assigned to a special troop put together to build morale. The 'Circus', as it was known, was comprised of a former professional boxer, professional wrestlers, a war hero famed for killing eighteen Germans with only a bayonet, and one very unusual clergyman. Woodbine Willie entered fully into the mission of the circus, often sparring with the professional boxer or clowning with the wrestlers. But it was an unusual warm-up act for a preacher and, aware of the incongruity, he would often start his sermons by asking: 'What the hell is the Church doing here?'

Woodbine Willie never used his increasing fame and notoriety to get him out of dangerous duties. Even the birth of his first son, Patrick, did nothing to weaken his resolve to serve on the frontlines. Before he had even met the child, he wrote:

The first prayer I want my son to learn to say for me is not "God keep daddy safe," but "God make daddy brave, and if he has hard things to do make him strong to do them." Life and death don't matter, Pat, my son; right and wrong do. Daddy dead is daddy still, but daddy dishonoured before God is something awful, too bad for words. I suppose you'd like to put in a bit about the safety too, old chap, and mother would. Well, put it in, but afterwards, always afterwards, because it does not really matter so much.[14]

In spite of this selfless bravery, Woodbine Willie did get to meet his son and to christen him in front of a large congregation in their home parish. He returned home for good in March 1919.

ITINERANT MINISTRY

Like so many others, Woodbine Willie returned to England disgusted by his initial support for the war and by the evils the conflict had unleashed. He was only sustained by the hope that the national soul-searching that followed the horrors of war might provide an opportunity for the Church to call the nation back to Christ.

Woodbine Willie went back to parish ministry at St Paul's, Worcester, and to family life with Emily and Patrick. He continued to combine traditional religious observance, including daily celebration of communion, with a commitment to practical service of the poor. Growing Sunday attendances at church and Sunday School and the creation of a new social centre were equally celebrated by Woodbine Willie. And he continued to witness to Christ in the most unlikely ways and in the most unlikely places. One former parishioner observed, 'He probably converted more people over pints of beer than anywhere else.'[15]

However, away from the joy of family life and the encouragement of growth at St Paul's, the country was in trouble. Woodbine Willie continued to hope that the war, for all its unimaginable horrors, might present the Church with an opportunity. He wrote:

> I am persuaded that it is a tremendous opportunity, born of England's agony, which we must take or be traitors to a trust – the most awful trust ever put in the hands of a Christian nation. Thousands who never thought of religion before are groping after the Truth. We must make them hear, through the agony of the nation, the call of Christ. Everything depends on how England receives home the

survivors of this awful conflict. The war will not do it by itself, but it is a great chance – a great chance if Christian people at home will take it.[16]

But, perhaps unsurprisingly, the aftermath of war was a downward spiral rather than revival. In tandem with spiritual decline, an economic crisis was developing. Huge numbers of returning soldiers found themselves without work and without hope.[17]

Woodbine Willie was identified as one of the few clergymen with the profile and skills to make a difference. By 1920 his reputation as a war hero, a speaker and an author were bringing him to prominence, including being made chaplain to King George V. His spellbinding oratory was frequently celebrated in the press. A terse report on a Good Friday sermon delivered in a London theatre ran: 'A vast crowd. Woodbine Willie. Men and women in tears.' Another relating to a sermon in York Minster observed: 'It was a brilliant sermon, plentifully relieved by flashes of humour and quick blows straight from the shoulder, but in depth and constructive thought making a very distinctive advance in the development of this modern prophet.'[18]

In 1921 Woodbine Willie was appointed 'messenger', a mixture of travelling evangelist and itinerant spokesperson, of the Industrial Christian Fellowship (ICF). It was a natural fit because the ICF's objectives closely resembled Woodbine Willie's own passions: To draw more working men and women into the Church, to help business and industry leaders to improve relations with and conditions of their workers without conflict and to work for a more just society. The new position meant leaving the parish of St Paul's. The congregation were downcast at being left behind by their beloved Rector but their devotion to Woodbine Willie and his family was evident in the kind speeches, gifts and cheques with which they sent them on their way.

In fact the Studdert Kennedy family did not leave Worcester. Emily and Patrick and, later, two further sons, Christopher (b. 1922) and Michael (b. 1927), continued to live in the city. Woodbine Willie himself divided his time between itinerant ministry for the ICF; the leadership of a small City of London church (offered to him by the Anglican hierarchy not to demand much of his time but as a source of financial provision for the family); and two days each week spent with the family in Worcester. Obviously there were costs involved in this complicated pattern of living. One biographer of Woodbine Willie noted at the beginning of his account, 'It will become clear that the man and his work would not have been possible except at the cost of considerable sacrifice on the part of both Geoffrey Studdert Kennedy and his wife, of their personal and family life. This cost they willingly faced together as part of the price which God demands of those who share a prophet's calling.'[19]

The label 'prophet' was increasingly frequently applied to Woodbine Willie by this stage in his ministry. His itinerant preaching and speaking took him abroad to the USA and Canada as well as all around the British Isles. And his voice came to be heard as one of great importance and of radical challenge to all parts of society.

Alongside his speaking, he wrote furiously, sometimes employing a secretary to take down his words as they travelled by car or train from city to city. A stream of books poured out of him. Wartime publications like *Rough Rhymes of a Padre*, *Rough Talks by a Padre* and *The Hardest Part* were followed in the aftermath of war by impassioned pleas for change, including: *Lies!*, *Democracy and the Dog Collar* and *Food for the Fed Up*. Later he published more reflective writings, often focused on particular passages of Scripture: *The Wicket Gate*, *The Word and the Work*, *The Warrior, the Woman and the Christ* and a novel about love and marriage, *I Pronounce Them*. Sadly, his passionate devotion to the people took its toll on his health.

By 1929, when he was 45 years old, his constant travelling and speaking had weakened him and worsened his asthma. In the spring of that year the whole family was struck down with illness, possibly due to a 'flu epidemic. But Woodbine Willie was committed to a series of Lent talks in Liverpool and was anxious not to let his hosts down. Once Emily had assured him that the family would cope without him, he set out in spite of his own ill health. Tragically, his illness worsened on the road and developed into pneumonia upon arrival in Liverpool. Emily was summoned and was driven to Liverpool by a friend but Woodbine Willie was unconscious by the time of her arrival. He died early in the morning of 8 March 1929 without having had the opportunity to say goodbye to either his wife or his sons.

His funeral back home in Worcester was a civic occasion. Workers took time off and the unemployed walked for miles to line the streets as the hearse passed by. Obituaries explained why these often forgotten men and women flocked to pay their respects:

> *The unhappy and the disinherited, the failures of this world and the buffeted seldom had a more heartening and valiant champion than Studdert Kennedy.*
> **The Daily Telegraph**

> *A man of intense vitality, glowing with compassionate sympathy, tortured by pity for human suffering and feeling that he had a message for mankind, he gave himself with it, with an utterly reckless and unselfish generosity. May he rest in peace.*
> **The Liverpool Echo**[20]

In addition to the ordinary people, many ecclesial and political dignitaries from all around the country came to Worcester to mourn his passing. Soon afterwards a group of his friends, including some of the most prominent churchmen of the time, published a book of reminiscences. In that volume, J.K. Mozley spoke for many when he wrote this epitaph:

[Woodbine Willie was] a great seeker after God, deeply devoted to his Master, passionately sincere, one to whom personal religion was the complete and only answer to the perversity of human wills, and [friends] reverence the memory of one whose greatest power lay in unfolding the love of God by speech and action, and in helping individual men and women to find the meaning and the glory, the purpose and the joy of life, in that surrender to the all-pervading presence of God which for him gave earth the character of heaven.[21]

We have seen how Woodbine Willie's sharp mind and soft heart made him an inspiring figure. His preaching, his writing and, above all, the life he lived, presented a prophetic hope to a generation terribly in need of encouragement. Moreover, in spite of his early death, he left behind a remarkable legacy in his example, his poetry and his prose. We will explore this legacy – the wisdom of Woodbine Willie – in the remaining chapters of this book.

CHAPTER 3

THE THOUGHT OF WOODBINE WILLIE

I believe that Woodbine Willie's wisdom, which we will go on to consider in some detail in the later parts of this book, has unusual power to speak into our lives, particularly where we struggle with doubt, confusion and disappointment. His practical wisdom flowed out of a deeper pool of theological reflection.

Woodbine Willie was never clever for cleverness sake. He was less than complimentary about professional philosophers and theologians, doubting their ability to communicate Christian truth to ordinary men and women:

> What can save the ordinary man from damning his soul and destroying his world? The piping of professors? The books of the philosophers? The knowledge of the scientists?

Vague goodwill and good-nature? You cold-blooded saints of the study, have you ever walked in the streets? Have you ever lived? Only a passion can conquer a passion – we must have God.[1]

Nonetheless, his desire to develop an alternative way of thinking about God which could 'save the ordinary man' required challenging theology.

A MANIFESTO

A passage from Woodbine Willie's book, *Lies!*, can be read as his intellectual manifesto. It was published in 1919, less than a year after the end of the First World War, at a time when all the old certainties, social and spiritual, had been shaken and were collapsing:

The world is out on the open sea exposed to every wind. And I am out on the open sea with it, but I do not care because there is One who walks beside me and before me and behind me, and God, who caused the light to shine out of darkness, has shined into my heart to give the light of the knowledge of the glory of God in the face of Jesus Christ. We are called upon, the Church is called upon, to go out on to the open sea with Christ, leaving behind the snug homes of patent infallibilities which the guns have battered into dust, and follow Him until we find the truth.

We are not in complete darkness. We are not without a Guide. Theology changes, but religion remains. To fold your hands and say, "God knows best," to take refuge in unreal platitudes, is to cower away from the light that God, through the prayers of the saints, through the courage of the scientists, through the cunning of inventors, and through the tireless patience of the thinkers, has been giving down the ages. The task of the Church and of her children, which is peculiarly her task and peculiarly theirs, is to gather up from every corner of the world all the light that can be found and set it blazing on this great problem of evil, in order to find the best partial solution for the children of our day, and the one which will provide the surest foundation for the complete solution which the passage of the ages, under God, will bring to light. We must seek for light in every corner of God's universe, never forgetting it is God's universe, and that in it we can find revelation of Himself. We must go down to life's dirtiest and dingiest depths, and up to its fairest and most fearful heights; we must face all the facts – the facts that make us shudder and the facts that make us laugh, the beauty that makes us gasp with wonder and the ugliness that makes us shrink in horror, the good that makes us want to worship and the evil that makes us bow our heads in shame; we must look at them all, face them all, asking always, "What is God like" – the God who is Creator and Ruler of a universe like this? We must not do what we have done, invent a God and then make life to fit Him, blinding our eyes to what does not suit our purpose; creating an absolute by the negative process of subtracting all human limitations from the human being, and choosing what we consider limitations, and what we do not. An imaginary God may be very beautiful, but He will not stand the tears and terror, and the fires that are not quenched. We must have truth.[2]

Key phrases in this passage highlight central ideas from Scripture that are the building blocks of all of Woodbine Willie's thinking, for example:

The glory of God in the face of Jesus Christ

This phrase is taken from 2 Corinthians 4:6, which appears to be Woodbine Willie's favourite verse, recurring again and again in his writings:

For God, who said, 'Let light shine out of darkness,' made his light shine in our hearts to give us the light of the knowledge of God's glory displayed in the face of Christ.

Woodbine Willie takes us down some challenging paths and, possibly, he takes some wrong turns. But he is worth following because of his passionate commitment to Jesus Christ and his belief that it is in Jesus Christ that the true God is revealed.

Jesus Christ I know and love. He is splendid. I love His superb courage, His majestic patience, and His perfect love. I love His terrible wrath against all wrong, and His tender kindness to the weak. Tender as a woman and terrible as a thunderstorm, Jesus Christ, I know and love.[3]

To take refuge in unreal platitudes is to cower away from the light

Woodbine Willie did not write challenging and novel theology because he was an egotistic radical or an academic with a career to build. He felt that the experiences of the common men and women, in terrible war and disappointing peace, exposed the weakness of the old, traditional answers, rendered them incomprehensible and, therefore, useless. His intellectual journey was undertaken on behalf of these men and women, so often ignored by churchmen and theologians.

This great problem of evil seen in life's dirtiest and dingiest depths

Woodbine Willie's life and times meant that he had no choice but to wrestle with the great problem of evil. He was brave enough to look the darkness full in the face, confident that in Jesus, the light of the world, there was luminosity capable of dispelling that darkness.

> The supreme strength of the Christian faith is that it faces the foulest and filthiest of life's facts in the crude brutality of the Cross, and through them sees the Glory of God in the face of Jesus Christ.[4]

Light in every corner of God's universe especially at its fairest and most fearful heights

One of the characteristics of Woodbine Willie's thought for which I am most grateful is the emphasis on the unity of all of life and experience. For the follower of Jesus Christ, there is no sacred/secular divide. The whole world is God's world and we should expect to find Him revealed in science as well as religion, in popular culture as well as church tradition. We worship and serve God in our Monday to Friday jobs as much if not more than in our Sunday celebrations.

We must not ... invent a God

Woodbine Willie's project was radical, challenging and sometimes unsettling because he believed that much of our habitual thinking about God is a kind of idolatry, a projection of our own concepts onto God. He argued that we often start with a picture of the human and then use the 'negative process of subtracting all human limitations' from that starting point in order to create a superhuman entity we name 'God'. However, this product of human intellect and imagination is not the true God who is revealed in Jesus Christ.

A SHARP MIND WRESTLING WITH GOD

From the earliest days of Woodbine Willie's ministry, his intellectual restlessness and quest for more satisfactory answers led to his testing the limits of conventional orthodoxy. During his curacy in Rugby his sermons regularly generated controversy. The Rector of Rugby, his boss, once told him: 'Kennedy ... I can stand one heresy from you each Sunday, but I cannot and will not stand two.' Apparently this stern admonition reduced Kennedy 'to guffaws of laughter and promises of amendment'.[5]

However, it was amidst the carnage of the Western Front that his thinking really developed. It was there that the questions that had long troubled him became truly unavoidable: 'That is the way with war. It shouts and bawls its questions at you. It throws them at you stark, raw, quivering, and all shot through with pain.'[6] The boldest statement of Woodbine Willie's signature thought is found in his book *The Hardest Part*, which was written in the trenches of the Western Front and published in the summer of 1918, before the end of the war. The book uses the questions of the soldiers he had learned to love and respect as its starting point, particularly their question 'What is God like?'

The Hardest Part divided its readers. The writer of the foreword, Woodbine Willie's friend and mentor the Dean of Worcester, Rev William Moore Ede, said:

Some may disapprove of what he has written and dissent from his conclusions, but they will profit by reading the book and learning how an earnest man endeavours to do for the British soldier what the writer of the book of Job and the prophet Isaiah endeavoured to do for the men of their times.[7]

Woodbine Willie himself noted in a postscript that 'Some very wise and good people have been hurt by what I have written.'[8]

SO, WHAT WAS SO DISTURBING?

In *The Hardest Part* Woodbine Willie pulled no punches in highlighting the challenge the First World War presented to the traditional Christian belief in an omnipotent God of love. 'God in history' is a particularly important chapter and it starts:

> In a German concrete shelter. Time, 2.30a.m. All night we had been making unsuccessful attempts to bring down some wounded men from the line. We could not get them through the shelling. One was blown to pieces as he lay on his stretcher.[9]

Of course, that particular tragedy, another father/husband/son obliterated, another child/wife/mother bereaved, was just one tiny part of the terrible whole. The armies of supposedly Christian nations were using all the technological and industrial resources at their disposal to destroy one another, elevating the horror of war to a qualitatively new level of mechanised destruction and a quantitatively new scale of casualties and fatalities. All the while, every combatant nation believed that God was on 'their' side. Woodbine Willie felt that this presented Christians with an extremely unpalatable dilemma:

> God is helpless to prevent war, or else he wills it and approves of it. There is the alternative. You pay your money and you take your choice.
>
> Christians in the past have taken the second alternative, and have stoutly declared that God wills war ... If you cling to God's absolute omnipotence, you must do it.

If God is absolutely omnipotent, He must will war, since war is and always has been the commonplace of history. Men are driven to the conclusion that war is the will of the Almighty God.

If it is true, I go morally mad. Good and evil cease to have any meaning ... If God wills war, then I am morally mad and life has no meaning. I hate war, and if God wills it I hate God and I am a better man for hating Him; that is the pass it brings me to.[10]

Unable to believe that God wills war, Woodbine Willie developed his most radical theology:

The truth is, that history drives one to the knowledge that God cannot be absolutely Almighty ... I would gladly die to kill the idea of the Almighty God ... I want to win the world to the worship of the patient, suffering Father God revealed in Jesus Christ.[11]

This was the pronouncement that discomforted and horrified many of Woodbine Willie's readers. In place of the traditional omnipotent King, the Almighty God ruling by decree from heaven, Woodbine Willie presented a suffering God at work in the world through a process of patient struggle and even failure. God had so far failed in His attempts to wean humanity off its reliance on war.

It's important to remember that Woodbine Willie's motivation was pastoral. He believed that the vision of an Almighty King seated on a heavenly throne, impervious to suffering, immune to the plight of humans, unmoved by war, provided no comfort for the petrified soldiers in the trenches and the worried families at home. When he was himself under heavy fire and terrified, he observed: 'It's funny how it is always Christ upon the Cross that comforts; never God upon a throne. One needs a Father, and a Father must suffer in His children's suffering. I could not worship the passionless potentate.'[12] His poem 'The Comrade God' makes the same point:

> Thou who dost dwell in depths of timeless being,
> Watching the years as moments passing by,
> Seeing the things that lie beyond our seeing,
> Constant, unchanged as aeons dawn and die;
>
> …
>
> Art Thou so great that this our bitter crying
> Sounds in Thine ears like sorrow of a child?
> Hast Thou looked down on centuries of sighing,
> And, like a heartless mother, only smiled?
>
> …
>
> Then, O my God, Thou art too great to love me,
> Since Thou dost reign beyond the reach of tears,
> Calm and serene as the cruel stars above me,
> High and remote from human hopes and fears.
>
> Only in Him can I find a home to hide me,
> Who on the Cross was slain to rise again;
> Only with Him, my Comrade God, beside me,
> Can I go forth to war with sin and pain.[13]

What are we to make of this radical theology of a suffering, struggling God who was unable to prevent the First World War? I would suggest that Woodbine Willie may be right in what he affirms but wrong in what he denies.

I think that Woodbine Willie has good grounds for arguing that God suffers, not just in the person of Jesus but also in the experience of the Father and the Spirit. He suffers not just at the moment of the crucifixion but continually down the ages, as He relates to a broken world and a lost humanity that He loves with a burning passion beyond our comprehension. And God has chosen, for the present, a way of working in the world that appears to us more like a painful struggle than a triumphant procession towards his kingdom come. Miracles are the exception not the rule. This might not surprise or unsettle you in the way that it surprised and unsettled Woodbine Willie's first readers. To believe that God suffers is now the consensus both for congregations in the churches and theologians in the universities. In fact, when I used to teach on the passibility of God (the technical term for the suffering of God) I struggled to convince a single student that there were problems with the idea that God suffers.

Today's Christians find it easy to dismiss the idea of an unchanging, unfeeling God as a hangover from the malign influence of Greek philosophy on Christian theology. When we read the Bible, we don't see a 'passionless potentate' or an 'unmoved mover', we see a God who is involved with His people, experiencing both joy and sadness in His relating to them. While God is not 'emotional' in the human sense, moody like a teenager or driven by changing feelings, we see no need to consider the biblical portrayal as mere anthropomorphism (assigning human characteristics to God for poetic or rhetorical reasons). We understand it as telling us something true about the experience of God.

As I said earlier, while I believe Woodbine Willie was right in what he affirmed, I think he was wrong in what he denied. In spite of his strong words in the paragraphs quoted above, I think Woodbine Willie still believes that God is omnipotent and almighty in the ways that matter. When Woodbine Willie denied the omnipotence of God, I think he was denying only an exaggerated caricature of omnipotence.

This caricature may be illustrated by this question: Can an omnipotent being create a stone too heavy for him to lift? Clearly it's a paradox: if the being can't create the stone impossible to lift there's something he can't do and he's not omnipotent. If he can create the impossibly heavy stone but, therefore, can't lift it, then there's something he can't do and he's not omnipotent! Of course, this point is not as straightforward as it first seems. No useful account of omnipotence requires God to be able to create stones he can't lift, any more than it requires Him to be able to do logically impossible things like creating square circles.

If we should not expect God to do the logically impossible then it may be just as nonsensical to expect God to create a world able to sustain free human beings, yet to exclude from that world the possibility of those free human beings choosing to act in ways that cause suffering for themselves and others, even the truly horrible suffering caused by war. If, as seems reasonable, true love cannot be coerced or compelled then God must give creatures a measure of freedom if they are to love Him. Unfortunately, it may be that freedom to love God and others logically requires freedom to reject God and others.

We can probably agree with Woodbine Willie that:

Human strife is not God's method, but His problem – a problem that arises from absolute but temporary necessities inherent in the task of creation. Strife and warfare arise from the limitation which the God of Love had to submit to in order to create spiritual personalities worthy to be called His sons. War is the crucifixion of God, not the working of His will.[14]

Nevertheless, why might God take such a risk and create a world where war is possible?

In Hebrews 12:2, we are told that Jesus Christ endured the agony of the cross for the joy that was set before Him. As Jesus had known perfect fellowship with God even before His incarnation, we can guess that the joy He looked forward to was the joy of an eternal fellowship that included His redeemed human brothers and sisters. The Father God's ultimate purpose is a vast community of men and women ('spiritual personalities') who are free to love Him and enjoy Him for all eternity ('to be called His sons [and daughters]'). In the words of the book of Revelation (Rev. 7:9, ESV):

> *a great multitude that no one could number, from every nation, from all tribes and peoples and languages, standing before the throne and before the Lamb ...*

In order to achieve His purpose, God creates a world where free humans can choose to love and serve Him and love and serve one another. A necessary consequence of this is a world where free human beings can choose to reject God and attempt to dominate one another. In such a world, war would always be possible. By emphasising human freedom (free will), we can say that God does not actively 'will' war in the way Woodbine Willie found so objectionable but might have reason to allow it. If God is understood to be a suffering, struggling God (rather than a self-satisfied monarch on a distant throne), we recognise that He takes upon Himself the worst of the suffering. What's more, and this is very important, He takes upon Himself the responsibility for one day ending the suffering.

Once again this seems to be Woodbine Willie's own position. He did not consider his radical theology a counsel of despair. He did not lose the hope that God would eventually bring His plans to fulfilment. His faith remained strong even as he stared out on the barren desolation of no man's land:

> Poor old patient mother earth, with all your beauty battered into barrenness by man's insanity. He who made you is not dead, though crucified afresh. Some day He will rise again for you, and all this wilderness that man has

made will blossom like the rose, and this valley will laugh with laughter of summer woods and golden grain, and cottage homes in whose bright gardens children play at peace and unafraid.[15]

At the end of *The Hardest Part*, while war still raged, he could affirm the creedal confession:

I can still stand facing East whence comes the Dawn, and say "I believe in God the Father Almighty," and in those glorious words confess my faith that the final Victory of God is as sure, nay, surer than the rising of tomorrow's sun. God is suffering His agony now, but the day will come when His agony and ours will be ended, and we shall sing our praise to the triumphant God of love.[16]

Given this statement of faith, I think it is best to understand Woodbine Willie's apparent rejection of the omnipotence of God as exaggeration or hyperbole, motivated by his abhorrence of the suffering he witnessed and his desire to make an important point. Certainly, we can recognise in his approach something of use in our own struggles with suffering.

If God has limited Himself, restricting His normal mode of acting in the world to a patient working from within, then I do not need to think that God actively wills the horrors of war, or illness, or rejection, or bereavement. If God continues to suffer, much as human parents suffer because of the pain of their children, then God is close to me in my difficulty, not distant on His throne in heaven. If God retains His omnipotence, His ultimate victory is still assured and I can have hope for the future in spite of pain in the present.

Nonetheless, we must always remember that we are severely limited by our intellectual capacities and our earthbound perspective. The thoughts and ways of God will always remain beyond us. With Woodbine Willie, we can cling to the hope that the ultimate purpose of God is so wonderful that we will one day recognise that what has been gained was worth the very great cost. But in this life, we will never find a truly satisfactory answer to the problem of how an omnipotent, loving God can allow horrendous suffering. In the presence of real suffering, the best answer to the question 'why?' is often silence or the honest admission that we don't know.

CHAPTER 4

THE WISDOM OF WOODBINE WILLIE:

FINDING THE MEANING OF LIFE IN A JOURNEY OF WONDER, VISION AND VENTURE

Try this 'thought experiment': imagine you are offered the chance to spend the rest of your life encased in a virtual reality apparatus. You will never move from the confines of the machine, you will never see the real world, you will never touch another human being, but, within the virtual world, you will never experience pain and you will have access to any pleasure and any experience you could ever desire. Would you take up that offer? Experiments show that the vast majority of people would not. As well as pleasure, we want our lives to have *meaning*. It seems that the desire to make a difference, to perform valuable service of some kind, is hardwired into the human psyche. Woodbine Willie believed that humans were created to transform the world. He thought the answer to the question of the meaning of life was to be found in a journey we can all take - from **wonder**, to **vision** and **venture**.

"He maketh me to lie down in green pastures,
He leadeth me beside the still waters"

The very beauty of this picture may only serve to hide from us the depths of its meaning. We seem to see the shepherd walking before his flock through fields decked out with green and gold and all the glory of a generous God, coming at last to the silent pool with the reflection of the sky sleeping in its heart, and it seems as though it were for the glory of the summer and the sleeping beauty of the pool that the sheep followed the shepherd. And, indeed, it is for that reason that many do seek the Good Shepherd. They think of religion not as a necessity but as a luxury, not as life but as a kind of addition to life which it is very nice to have but which we could quite do without. But it is not for the green and gold of summer fields that the sheep seeks to find them, but because they are good to eat. It is not for the sleeping beauty in the heart of silent waters that the flock follows on to find them, but because they are good to drink. It is not luxury that they ask of the shepherd, it is the bare necessities. And we cannot make too sure of this, that religion, communion with God, is not luxury but a necessity for the soul. We must have God.

We are hungry headed, hungry hearted, hungry souled, and this intellectual, emotional and spiritual hunger is as tyrannous and terrible if it be not satisfied as the hunger of the body. Many of us are not conscious fully of our hunger of the head and yet it is there. Life lies spread before us like a book - a strange and wonderful book written in characters that we slowly learn to understand - and as year by year we turn its pages over, the need to find a meaning in what we read becomes more and more an imperative necessity in our lives. It is literally maddening to be compelled to read a book when here and there are lines, perhaps lines of perfect beauty, which we can understand and which make us certain that there is a meaning hidden in the whole, and yet, no sooner do our hopes rise high and our eyes begin to shine than we come across a passage which is utterly incomprehensible, and worse than that, looks as though it had been written either by a villain or a fool.

This is like life. It challenges us continually. Challenges our curiosity, our courage, our self-respect. It flings a thousand questions at us and until we begin to die, and we begin to die when we begin to give it up, there is a passionate desire within us to answer the challenge and find the meaning of life. This is the hunger of the head, the hunger for truth and reality, and it must be fed.

Now whatever be the truth that the mind seeks it can only move towards it along one road, and on that road there are three stages. The first is wonder, the second is vision, and the third is venture. There is no other road to the palace of truth but that.[1]

This text is taken from a final collection of Woodbine Willie's writings published after his death in the book, *The New Man in Christ*. In this meditation, he reflects on the famous Psalm 23. He observes that the beautiful imagery of the Psalm, the green pastures and still waters, can lead us to read it with luxury in mind. Today, we might be reminded of travel agency brochures, substituting gently waving palm trees for the green pastures and a glittering, aquamarine sea for the still waters. That couldn't be more wrong, argues Woodbine Willie. This Psalm is not about luxury but about the necessities of life. The sheep look to the shepherd for the basics – grass to eat and water to drink. We should look to the Good Shepherd in the same way: 'communion with God is not luxury but a necessity for the soul. We must have God.' 'We are hungry headed, hungry hearted, hungry souled' and it is this hunger that, eventually, drives us to ask questions of the world around us and to contemplate the meaning of life. It is these questions that lead us, again and again, to God who alone has the capacity to offer us fullness of life.

WONDER, VISION AND VENTURE

If we can lift our eyes from the screens that command our attention and tear our minds free from the constant burble of the media and the chatter of our friends, we are sure to be driven to **wonder** by the world around us.

Sometimes we wonder negatively – which is to say, we doubt. We wonder whether any love can be worth the agony of loss – be it the loss be of the girlfriend of a few months to another man, or the spouse of many decades to cancer. We wonder about pain endured by the innocent and doubt whether any future bliss can compensate – the children displaced and orphaned by natural disaster, the women raped and abused or the men brutalised by conflict or discarded by the economy. These are the chapters in life's book that look as though they had been 'written by a villain or a fool'. We ask: Could a good God really be responsible for this messed-up world?

At other times the world seems 'wonder-filled' in a much more positive sense. An unexpected piece of good fortune leaves us feeling graced, as if we've received the world's blessing. A glimpse of natural beauty can cause us to catch our breath and make us want to worship. The cheeky smile of a beloved child can cause our hearts to swell with gratitude. But who is blessing us, who should we worship, to whom do we owe our gratitude?

For Woodbine Willie, veteran of the horrors of the trenches, pastor to the slum dwellers, and lover of the natural world, the questions posed by life all pointed to one thing, to one man, to a Jewish man hanging on a Roman cross. Christian faith begins with the revelation of the glory of God in the face of Jesus Christ (2 Cor. 4:6). This is the **vision** that is at the heart of the Christian life. This is the Christian answer to the problem of a beautiful but broken world. In Jesus Christ we find the One who can mend the brokenness that our hearts protest against. In Jesus Christ we encounter the One who has poured out blessings on us, who is worthy of our worship, who deserves our gratitude.

Woodbine Willie believed it was impossible to see a vision of Jesus Christ without, simultaneously, receiving a call to live for Him by serving others. Thus wonder leads to questions to which the answer is the vision of Jesus Christ, and the vision leads to the great **venture** of life - a calling to show the world Jesus, to transform the world into the kind of place that you could imagine Him ruling, into the kind of place that reflects who He is, and the kind of place that would bring pleasure to His heart.

For Woodbine Willie both wonder and wondering, rejoicing and doubting, could be the starting points of a journey, in fact the start of *the* journey. Woodbine Willie taught that the meaning of life was to be found on this journey towards the God revealed in the face of Jesus Christ. In the remaining parts of this book we will follow the path he laid out for us. We will travel from **wonder**, through **vision** and then into **venture**.

REFLECTION

It's common to go through life with barely any attention paid to the persons, places and things beyond our immediate circle of concern and responsibility. It's tempting for us to suppress our deepest questions, doubts and fears. The frantic pace of contemporary life and the constant availability of myriad forms of distraction make both these evasions easy – most of the time. For many of us, questions only surface in times of stress and crisis. But if our questions are the beginning of a journey towards God, it's much healthier to draw them into the light and address them in moments of confidence and calm.

Many of us only have the time to really see the world around us in times of quiet – freely chosen rest like holidays or imposed inaction like illnesses, for example. But if our attending to the world is an important part of our discipleship, it's much healthier to learn to pay attention to the world around us, the light and the shadow, all of the time.

To that end, we might spend a few minutes considering the following questions:

- What do you find to be most wonder-full about the world and human experience?
- What fills you with gratitude and makes you want to rejoice and worship?
- What aspects of the 'book of human life' appear to you to have been written by a villain or a fool?
- What makes you doubt the goodness of God and, perhaps, even question the existence of God?

READ PSALM 23

The LORD is my shepherd, I lack nothing. He makes me lie down in green pastures, he leads me beside quiet waters, he refreshes my soul. He guides me along the right paths for his name's sake. Even though I walk through the darkest valley, I will fear no evil, for you are with me; your rod and your staff, they comfort me.

You prepare a table before me in the presence of my enemies. You anoint my head with oil; my cup overflows. Surely your goodness and love will follow me all the days of my life, and I will dwell in the house of the LORD for ever.

WONDER

Read through the psalm picking out the wonder-full images that reflect the beauty and good things of the world all around us. If you were to write a wonder-full prayer-poem like this, using imagery taken from your daily life and experience, what would you write about?

Then, read through the psalm again picking out the dark and frightening images that reflect natural human fears and the reality of life in a fallen world. If you were to write an honest prayer-poem like this, using examples drawn from your own doubts and fears, what would you incorporate?

VISION

Read through the psalm one more time, identifying the activity of our Lord God, the Good Shepherd. What does God provide? What does God's presence offer? What hope does the psalmist find in God?

If you were the psalmist, writing in hope and trust, what would you expect God to provide for you and your life?

VENTURE

Finally, reflect on the phrase, 'leads me in paths of righteousness'. In the great venture of your life, where do you currently believe God is leading you? What acts of righteousness is he calling you to perform? How will you shine like a star in your generation (Phil. 2:15)?

PRAYER

Father God, help me to be attentive to the world around me, to recognise Your presence and Your protection, and to venture to live my life for Your glory. Amen.

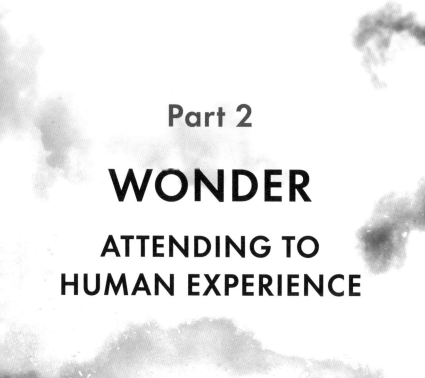

Part 2

WONDER

ATTENDING TO HUMAN EXPERIENCE

CHAPTER 5

WHAT IS THE NATURE OF NATURE?

If you are of a certain disposition, you might have been stopped in your tracks by a particularly intense sunset. You might have had your breath catch in your throat at the sudden opening-up of an awesome mountain vista. You might have felt your heart swell at the miracle of a small flower bursting into life out of the tiniest crack in the concrete jungle. Sometimes beauty leads us to wonder what lies behind the surface of the world – what is the nature of nature? Woodbine Willie was a life-long lover of the natural world. Even amid the desolation of no man's land, its unutterable beauty could creep up and overwhelm him. In this passage he explores one way of understanding the wonder that natural beauty inspires.

June 15th 1917

In a shell hole near the pill-box which was B.H.Q. [Battalion Head Quarters]. The dawn of day after a battle. All night the evacuation of the wounded had gone on without a stop. There were many casualties.

I don't believe I could carry another one to save my life. Lord, how my shoulders ache. I wish I were stronger. It's a good thing there are no more to carry. I wonder – will that last chap live? His thigh seemed all mash when we pulled him in. It was a beastly job. He cried for mercy and we had to drag on just the same. He is strong though, a splendid body all broken up. It's quiet now, only for those 5.9's over on the right. They never stop. I'm glad to sit and think. How I do love quiet. What a perfect morning it is. All the sky burns red with the after-blush of dawn, and here I seem surrounded by a soft grey sea of mist. What unutterable beauty there is in Nature. No wonder artists despair. God's fruits. I suppose the first of all God's fruits by which we may know Him is the world of Nature. Nature drives a man to belief in something, or rather some one, behind it all ...

Nature is one of God's fruits by which we have to know Him. I know it is hard to see in Nature what God is; its many voices seem to contradict one another. Its tenderness and cruelty, its order and its chaos, its beauty and its ugliness, make discords in its song and mar the music of its message to the soul of man. There is much truth in the charge that Nature is red in tooth and claw. It is hard to see God in a cobra or a shark.

Nevertheless, the heart of the ordinary man will always turn away from these things and come back to the glory of a summer dawn and worship the Maker of it. "The Veiled Being," Wells calls Him, and He may be that; but still I stretch my hands out toward the veil and worship Him in gratitude, although I cannot see His face. I've got to worship Him. It isn't my intellect that wants Him, it's my "me," my innermost essential me. I want to paint or draw or put into words some expression of my love and praise. It calls and grips. For me the world will always be a vast and starlit temple where every bush and flower flames with God, and I believe in that I am just an extension of the average man.

Still, there is truth in the statement that Nature's God must always be an unknown God.[1]

Moral beauty and ugliness can coexist in each one of us. As a species, we have developed weapons technologies capable of reducing our planet to radioactive rubble and yet we also have capacities that mirror the creative genius of God. Artists have coaxed beauty from the most unpromising materials and engineers have transformed barren wildernesses into fertile farmland. In this respect, we resemble the equally complex material world we inhabit. The gentle ocean swell can mutate into a tsunami. The sun that coaxes wildflowers from the earth in an English springtime can leave a parched desert in Africa.

But Woodbine Willie argues that humans have a tendency to turn away from the ugliness and orient themselves towards the beauty in nature. 'The heart of the ordinary man will always ... come back to the glory of a summer dawn and worship the Maker of it.' He explores this tendency further in his poetry:

SO I DREAM

There is more behind the sunshine
Than the sun,
Fiercely flaming in the sky,
As the ages dawn and die,
Like a sneering sightless eye,
Seeing none.
There's a voice my spirit knows,
In the sunset's gold and rose,
And the purple afterglows,
When it's done.

There is speech behind the silence
Of the night,
When the myriad array,
Sweeping down the Milky Way,
Marches on to dawning day
Silver white;
When the velvet of the air,
Like some lovely woman's hair,
Drives the heavy eyes of care
Out of sight.

There's a message in the music
Of the deep,
When great Ocean's heaving swells,
Like God's big cathedral bells,
Boom their solemn-sounding knells,
As they sweep,
In an ecstasy of pride,
At the flowing of the tide,
Over those who fought and died,
Fast asleep.

There is love behind the splendour
Of the spring,
When the weary winter dies
And the Lord with laughing eyes
Bids the trembling world arise,
Whispering,
"Did ye think that God was dead?
Nay my blood is warm and red,
And there is no death to dread –
Come and sing."

Lord, I pray Thee give my spirit
Eyes to see,
Through the things of time and space,
All the glories of Thy grace,
The commandment of Thy face,
Bidding me
Follow on where Thou hast trod;
Though I share the grief of God,
Give me strength to sweat my blood,
Lord, for Thee.[2]

If Woodbine Willie is right, he's put his finger on a remarkable aspect of the human experience of the world. He suggests that the 'ordinary' or 'average' human being considers the beauty and order in the world to be somehow good and right, while 'turning away' from the ugliness and violence as somehow wrong and distorted.

It's a response that makes no sense if you're an atheist. Most atheists take the world to be amoral – not good or bad – in all its various guises. It is simply the unplanned, unexpected result of random processes playing out over endless aeons. But it's a response to the world that makes perfect sense if you believe the Christian story. It would seem that humans resonate with the biblical narrative of a good creation that has been marred and distorted by a fall away from God. It would appear that we yearn instinctively for the renewal of creation, the restoration of its intrinsic goodness and, indeed, its elevation to new heights of glory under the Lordship of Christ (Rom. 8:18–25).

REFLECTION

Research has shown that natural beauty is the most common trigger for the kinds of experiences that even non-believers are driven to describe as spiritual or transcendent. Many Christians find nature a place of encounter with God. In the Reflection section of this chapter, we will consider the way in which the beauty of nature can facilitate our encounter with God and what it might teach us about God.

READ PSALM 19

The heavens declare the glory of God; the skies proclaim the work of his hands. Day after day they pour forth speech; night after night they reveal knowledge. They have no speech, they use no words; no sound is heard from them. Yet their voice goes out into all the earth, their words to the ends of the world. In the heavens God has pitched a tent for the sun. It is like a bridegroom coming out of his chamber, like a champion rejoicing to run his course. It rises at one end of the heavens and makes its circuit to the other; nothing is deprived of its warmth.

The law of the LORD is perfect, refreshing the soul. The statutes of the LORD are trustworthy, making wise the simple. The precepts of the LORD are right, giving joy to the heart. The commands of the LORD are radiant, giving light to the eyes.

The fear of the LORD is pure, enduring for ever. The decrees of the LORD are firm, and all of them are righteous.

They are more precious than gold, than much pure gold; they are sweeter than honey, than honey from the honeycomb. By them your servant is warned; in keeping them there is great reward. But who can discern their own errors? Forgive my hidden faults. Keep your servant also from wilful sins; may they not rule over me. Then I will be blameless, innocent of great transgression.

May these words of my mouth and this meditation of my heart be pleasing in your sight, LORD, my Rock and my Redeemer.

Psalm 19 is the classic expression of what theologians sometimes call 'general revelation' – the revelation of God which is accessible to all people through their encounter with the natural world which to some degree reflects and witnesses to its Creator. Here we see Scripture confirming the insight of Woodbine Willie and corroborating our experience of encountering God in nature – 'the heavens declare the glory of God' (v1).

Take a few minutes to read and reflect on Psalm 19:1–6.

- Do these verses resonate with your own experience of nature?
- What kind of God do the heavens, sky, day, night and the sun speak of to you?

It is important to note that this is, primarily, not a psalm about nature but a psalm about the 'law of the LORD'. It is the law of the Lord that is perfect, the testimony of the law that is sure (v7). In this context, the law corresponds to what theologians sometimes refer to as 'special revelation' – the revelation of God that is found only in Scripture and, especially, in Scripture's witness to the life, death and resurrection of Jesus Christ. Without this special revelation, nature can never lead us to a true image of God. Human experience of the natural world coupled with human imagination will only ever be able to construct idols (Rom. 1:18–25). As Woodbine Willie said, 'Nature's God must always be an unknown God'. In the language of these chapters, nature can cause us to 'wonder' but it is only in Jesus Christ that we are given a true 'vision' of God.

Take a few minutes to read and reflect on Psalm 19:7–14
Ask yourself:

- Are there any errors (v12) which have crept into my picture of God because of the fallen-ness of the natural world?
- Has suffering made me feel that God is distant and uncaring?
- Have the excesses of our consumer culture led me to believe that the natural world doesn't matter to God and/or that God doesn't matter to the natural world?

FOR FURTHER REFLECTION

What was your experience of nature before you were a Christian?

- For example, were you drawn to its beauty or repelled by its cruelty?
- Did you experience it as 'creation' and wonder about the reality of a 'creator'?

- Or were you content with what science is able to tell us about a big bang and slow evolution over billions of years?
- Did nature play any part in your journey towards faith?

Does the natural world play a part in your Christian discipleship?

- Do you find it easier to encounter God outside or inside?
- Do you ever retreat into the countryside to walk and pray?
- Do natural history programmes on television inspire you to worship the creator of such wondrous complexity and diversity?
- Do magnificent mountains, restless oceans or limitless skies stretch your image of the majesty of God? Or do parasites and pandemics, tsunamis and tornadoes shake your confidence in the goodness of God?
- How might intentional immersion in the natural world, coupled with a firm grasp of Scripture, help you to grow in your understanding of who God is and what his purposes are for the world?

Have you had the opportunity to enjoy the natural world with non-Christian friends, colleagues and relatives?

- If so, have you noticed any difference between the way you experience nature and they experience it? Why might this be?
- Do you think they might be open to a Christian explanation of the complex – beautiful/ugly, flourishing/decaying – nature of nature as created good but fallen from grace?

- Are there ways in which some non-Christians' attitudes to the world challenge and convict us? Are they more protective of the environment than we are? Are they more willing to give up their own luxuries in order to guarantee there is plenty for others?
- Might our common experience of nature be a starting point for witness to the creator God revealed in Jesus Christ?

PRAYER

Creator God, I thank You for the beauty of Your world and for what it reveals of Your inventiveness and power. Help me to grow in understanding of You as I study Your revelation in nature and in Scripture. Amen.

CHAPTER 6

WHAT IS THE PURPOSE OF PLEASURE?

Humans have a complex array of senses that enable us to enjoy an incredible range of pleasurable sensations and experiences. We have aesthetic apparatus that allows us to appreciate great art, music and story. We have a sense of humour that can find comedy in the most unlikely circumstances and even in apparent misfortune. Yet none of these myriad pleasures can ever fully satisfy. We constantly find ourselves wanting more – more ice-cream, more sex, more music, more jokes. Woodbine Willie thought that our pleasures pointed beyond themselves, offering a tantalising glimpse of what might ultimately satisfy the restless human heart. As strange as it might seem, death is the clue.

In the midst of life we are in death, its shadow falls over everything.

'Twere heaven enough to fill my heart
If only one would stay,
Just one of all the million joys
God gives to take away.

If I could keep one golden dawn,
The splendour of one star,
One silver glint of yon bird's wing
That flashes from afar;

Lift ye up your hearts to God.

If I could keep the least of things
That make me catch my breath
To gasp with wonder at God's world
And hold it back from death,

It were enough; but death forbids.
The sunset flames to fade,
The velvet petals of this rose
Fall withered – brown – decayed.

O Grave, Where is Thy victory?
O Death, where is Thy sting?
Thy victory is ev'rywhere,
Thy sting's in ev'rything.

There is a stage in a small child's life, when one of its greatest joys is to be taken up by its father and swung in the air, and I can see now my own small son standing before me when I have just put him down, and saying, with shining eyes, "Do it again Daddy, do it again." And in him I see a picture of the whole world of men and women standing before the great All Father Who makes the sunset and the rose, and crying as they fade and fail, "Do it again Daddy, do it again" – always trying to recapture the ecstasy, and never quite succeeding. There is only one way by which we can ever capture, and hold fast for ever the joys that come and go, that is by capturing and holding fast the Father Himself from Whom they come. Always we must stand in a world of dying things and dying people crying out through our tears, "Do it again Daddy, do it again," until the moment comes when the Father reaches down, snatches us to His heart, and holds us there for ever.

The more we grow in the love of Beauty, Truth and Goodness, the more completely human we become, the more intense must grow our hunger for immortality and our abhorrence of death.[1]

The human heart and mind are restless, only ever momentarily satisfied, always moving on towards the next big thing. In our time, a vast industry of advertising has developed a million-and-one ways of accentuating this restlessness. But even if we could attain all the possessions our hearts desire and could receive from them all of the pleasures imaginable, what could they offer us in the face of death? 'Who dies with the most money wins' might, just conceivably, be as good a philosophy to build your life on as any other. But it has no answer to the irrefutable truth that 'you can't take it with you'.

In the passage we have just read, Woodbine Willie acknowledges this truth with a burst of poetry. In the poem he emphasises, simultaneously, the beauty and desirability of the natural world and our instinctive revulsion at its (and our) transience. He follows up with a brilliantly well-chosen illustration drawn from family life.

The child's pleasure in movement is genuine; a good, joyous expression of life and vitality. Physical pleasures are real. The material world that God made is good and the bodily existence he gave to humans is good. I don't want to imply that physical pleasures are only signposts to a more important spiritual realm. That would be an expression of the dualism that has plagued Christianity down the centuries and horrified Woodbine Willie. So the first purpose of pleasure is pleasure, a joyful celebration of the embodied existence given to us by God.

Given how much fun it is to be swung, the child's desire for repetition is entirely natural. But we know that were the father to keep swinging and swinging, the child would eventually become bored. It's something we all know from experience. There's a kind of built-in 'statute of limitation' on our physical pleasures. They can only satisfy us for a limited time. It is here that the brilliance of Woodbine Willie's choice of illustration becomes clear. It draws attention to the fact that there's something profound going on behind the simple, physical pleasure of the movement. The simple bodily pleasure can be enjoyed in a swing or on a rollercoaster. But here there is another component already included – the pleasure of physical intimacy. There is the affectionate, physical closeness of the child with his father.

Human relationships afford a pleasure that is complex enough to evolve continually over an entire lifetime. They have no 'statute of limitation' like simple physical pleasure. The father and son could continue relating through all the stages of life and there would still be more to learn about one another, more to love about one another, more to enjoy in one another. But then there's death. Woodbine Willie wrote this passage in the early 1920s. Tragically, he died just a few years later. He and his son, Patrick, had a very limited time together. Woodbine Willie never saw Patrick develop into an adult. Patrick never knew his father in old age. But even in the case of extreme long life, death (the great *non sequiter* of human existence) will have the final say.

The deeper the love, the better the quality of the relationship, the more keenly the loss is felt. This is the truth of the final line of the passage. So is there a purpose to pleasure that can transcend death?

Our experience of the natural world, the beauty of a sunset or of a rose, the exhilaration of embodied living and freedom of movement brings us pleasure. There is also the deeper more lasting pleasure to be found in human relationships, in the loving commitment that allows us to know one another deeply and to go on growing together, day after day, year after year, decade after decade. But none of these pleasures can survive the brutal intervention of death. The deeper purpose of pleasure is to cause our hearts to cry out for something that is stronger than death. The human heart instinctively recoils from death and rebels against it. We don't want the sunset to fade, the rose to decay or relationships to end. In other words, we long for a love that is stronger than death. Nothing less will satisfy.

In this passage, Woodbine Willie exposes the fact that every human heart is actually crying out for the Father whose embrace will never end. We need the strong arms of the 'great All Father' who can carry us not simply in a childhood game but through all the trials and tribulations of life. We need the only arms of love that can grip us tightly enough to hold us through and beyond death into eternity.

> There is only one way by which we can ever capture, and hold fast for ever the joys that come and go, that is by capturing and holding fast the Father Himself from Whom they come. Always we must stand in a world of dying things and dying people crying out through our tears, "Do it again Daddy, do it again," until the moment comes when the Father reaches down, snatches us to His heart, and holds us there for ever.

REFLECTION

The question of how to appropriately enjoy earthly pleasures, without turning them into destructive idols, was a common subject for Jesus' teaching to His followers.

We can tell that Jesus valued the physical and material world because He spent many years as a builder, He healed the sick and, most importantly, He rose from the dead not as an ethereal spirit but in a body (albeit a very special kind of body that we have not yet experienced). Jesus also celebrated physical pleasure by turning water into wine, comparing the kingdom of God to a huge party, and enjoying good food and good company – so much so that His enemies accused Him (unfairly) of being a glutton and a drunkard!

Here we are going to consider a passage from the most famous of Jesus' sermons – commonly known as the Sermon on the Mount.

READ MATTHEW 6:19–34

Do not store up for yourselves treasures on earth, where moths and vermin destroy, and where thieves break in and steal. But store up for yourselves treasures in heaven, where moths and vermin do not destroy, and where thieves do not break in and steal. For where your treasure is, there your heart will be also ...

No one can serve two masters. Either you will hate the one and love the other, or you will be devoted to the one and despise the other. You cannot serve both God and Money.

Therefore I tell you, do not worry about your life, what you will eat or drink; or about your body, what you will wear. Is not life more than food, and the body more than clothes? Look at the birds of the air; they do not sow or reap or store away in barns, and yet your heavenly Father feeds them. Are you not much more valuable than they? Can any one of you by worrying add a single hour to your life?

And why do you worry about clothes? See how the flowers of the field grow. They do not labour or spin. Yet I tell you that not even Solomon in all his splendour was dressed like one of these. If that is how God clothes the grass of the field, which is here today and tomorrow is thrown into the fire, will he not much more clothe you – you of little faith? So do not worry, saying, 'What shall we eat?' or 'What shall we drink?' or 'What shall we wear?' For the pagans run after all these things, and your heavenly Father knows that you need them. But seek first his kingdom and his righteousness, and all these things will be given to you as well. Therefore do not worry about tomorrow, for tomorrow will worry about itself. Each day has enough trouble of its own.

Lay up treasures in heaven (vv19–24, ESV)

- What images does Jesus use to make a similar point about the temporary nature of earthly pleasures in this passage?
- Do you have experience of pleasures that were destroyed or stolen from you? How did you react?
- Did the experience turn you towards God or away from God?

'Where your treasure is, there your heart will be also.' (v21, ESV)

- How does this observation of Jesus' play out in our lives and the lives of the people around us?
- What does a person whose heart is totally focused on earthly treasure look like?
- What do they live like?
- What does a person whose heart is totally focused on heavenly treasure look like?
- What do they live like?
- Which one do you most resemble?

'No one can serve two masters ... You cannot serve God and money.' (v24, ESV)

In our world, perhaps even more than in Jesus' time, money is the route to a vast range of physical pleasures. That's not necessarily a bad thing (as we will see when we talk about money at greater length in a later chapter). But while money might be a good servant, it is a bad master. Are there habits or practices that you employ to ensure that money doesn't rule your life?

Do not be anxious (vv25–34, ESV)

'Look at the birds ... consider the lilies' (vv26,28, ESV)

We have argued that the purpose of pleasure is to lead us to the realisation that what we really need is the love of God which is stronger than death. What this passage makes clear is that this is not the end of physical pleasure or of a satisfying life in this world. The birds of the air and the lilies of the field reap the benefits of a trusting dependence on God and he blesses them abundantly with all that they need. God also wants to bless his human children.

- What are the blessings which God has poured into your life?
- What are you most thankful for?
- What are the needs which continue to go unmet?
- Can you learn to set aside anxiety and trust that God will provide you with all the good things you need?

'But seek first the kingdom of God and his righteousness and all these things will be added to you.' (v33, ESV)
It is often a struggle to trust God to provide without descending into anxiety. This verse tells us that it is in refocusing our lives upon the kingdom that we can begin to achieve this. What actions might you take to ensure that your life is focused on the kingdom of God?

PRAYER

Heavenly Father, help me to put my passions and desires in right order so that in loving You and seeking Your kingdom I may also enjoy all the good things you have blessed us with. Amen.

Part 3

VISION

SEEING THE GLORY OF GOD IN THE FACE OF JESUS CHRIST

CHAPTER 7

WHAT IS GOD LOOKING FOR?

The previous chapters have focused on **wonder** – our experience of the world leads us to question what lies behind its natural beauty, to yearn for something permanent, something stronger than death. But human questioning and yearning can only ever afford a glimpse of truth and a glimmer of hope. Christianity is not about us going to look for God but about God coming looking for us. Christianity is unique in believing that religion is a movement from God to humanity. There is a short answer to the question, *what is God looking for?* That answer is *you*.

> The essence of the Christian revelation is that revelation of God as a coming God, a seeking God, a Good Shepherd Who seeks His sheep; a poor woman who seeks her lost coin, and leaves no least stone unturned to find it; a Father seeking for His sons; a Love that never ceases, and by its nature never could cease, to seek for perfect expression in man. Wherever and whenever there is the remotest chance of this living energy of Love breaking out into new and

more perfect forms of beauty, it will do so. Nothing keeps it back, not even sin. That, surely, is the whole essence of the Christian Truth – Not even sin. While we were yet sinners, Christ died for us. Before we repented, God loved us. Sin did estrange man from God; but it never has, and it never could, estrange God from man. God never waits for us to come to Him, God is for ever coming to us – He is the coming God.

Because in tender majesty
Thou cam'st to earth, nor stayed till we,
Poor sinners, stumbled up to thee,
I thank my God.

Because the Saviour of us all
Lay with the cattle in their stall,
Because the Great came to the small,
I thank my God.

Because upon a Mother's breast
The Lord of Life was laid to rest,
And was of the babes the liveliest,
I thank my God.

Because the Eternal Infinite
Was once that little naked Mite,
Because – O Love of Christmas night,
I thank my God!

... God is seeking you now. If for one single moment He could cease to seek you, the stars would fall, and the very mountains crumble into dust. He is seeking you, as He is seeking the dirtiest, meanest apology for a man that crawls upon the earth; and wherever He gets the shadow of a chance, He will succeed.[1]

At the beginning of the text quoted above, Woodbine Willie refers to three parables told by Jesus and recorded in Luke 15. The first two verses of that chapter provide the context for Jesus' telling of these stories. There is an accusation directed at Jesus by the proudly religious Pharisees. They are horrified because Jesus is spending his time with 'tax collectors and sinners'.

Woodbine Willie was a champion of the poor, the marginalised, the suffering, the men and women who were outside of polite society – the tax collectors and sinners of his time. He loved the bawdy songs and bustle of the public houses, the earthy humour and the rough comradeship of the soldiers. He frequently contributed to the commotion and the laughter with his own singing and joke telling.

Woodbine Willie was horrified by the way the Church seemed only to attract the well-off, the well-connected and the well-mannered. He believed that the Church made ordinary people feel that they had to scrub-up and become respectable before they would be acceptable to God. He hated this. He believed it was a lie and a complete betrayal of the gospel. In Luke 15, Jesus' response was to tell three stories about seeking and finding. Building upon these stories, Woodbine Willie preached the 'coming God', the God who does not sit upon a throne waiting for humans to come to Him but sets out to seek and to save that which was lost. He taught that God was on a quest.

All human cultures have celebrated the heroic quest for something of great beauty or great worth. Myths and sagas, novels and movies have depicted heroes searching for priceless treasures, laying siege to important cities, restoring royal honour. In these stories the object of the quest is always something of universally recognised beauty or value. For the stories to work, the audience must understand and identify with the drive that sends the hero out into the wilderness. They must share the hero's estimation of the value of the prize. The quest may be perilous but it cannot be illogical. The most prevalent and powerful stories of all are those of a prince on a quest to find his true love.

Christianity upsets the logic of these popular stories. As illustrated in Jesus' parables, Christianity makes the scandalous claim that the great prince *par excellence*, the very Lord of the Universe, would leave His kingdom in order to seek and to find any common human being. It seems absurd, what kind of madness would induce a great prince to risk all in order to seek 'the dirtiest, meanest apology for a man that crawls upon the earth'? Woodbine Willie has no doubts. It is the madness of a love so potent, so persistent that it is beyond our comprehension.

The Gospel narrative is the popular story turned on its head and made real. The great Prince of Peace leaves His kingdom and endures poverty in an insecure political backwater under foreign domination. The great Prince gives up all strength and power, even to the point of becoming a helpless baby dependent on His mother to meet every single need. As Woodbine Willie says, 'Because upon a Mother's breast, The Lord of Life was laid to rest ... I thank my God.'

And the life the Prince of Peace lives as He grows to maturity is the opposite of the normal stories. He does not wield the sword, raise an army, or conquer a swathe of territory. He willingly endures humiliation, including being betrayed and deserted by His closest friends. He suffers at the hands of powers that have not a fraction of His authority or might. And He dies in disgrace alongside common criminals, jeered at by contemptuous crowds.

Other religions have a kind of reasonableness. Fulfil these duties, obey these rules and perform these rituals. Strive and plead with the deity and, in his mercy, he might look down from his throne and permit you to draw near to him. He might even offer you a place in heaven. In contrast, Christianity is, in this sense, profoundly unreasonable. Christianity turns the whole structure upside down. It is *God* who puts in the effort. It is *God* who makes the first move. As Woodbine Willie quotes, 'while we were yet sinners, Christ died for us' (Rom. 5:8, ESV). This is the good news of Christianity, the gospel in its purest essence!

So again, what is God looking for? God is looking for *you*! Looking for you exactly as you are, regardless of the mess you're in or the mistakes you've made. Looking for you now, not waiting for you to straighten out your life or clean yourself up.

If for one single moment He could cease to seek you, the stars would fall, and the very mountains crumble into dust.

REFLECTION

In this chapter, I've presented the gospel as a story of a great Prince who left His kingdom on a quest. In line with the teaching of Scripture, including the parables of Luke 15, I've suggested that the Prince of Peace, the very Lord of the Universe, would have left His kingdom and engaged in this quest to save any member of the human race – even you, even me.

READ LUKE 15:1–32

Now the tax collectors and sinners were all gathering round to hear Jesus. But the Pharisees and the teachers of the law muttered, 'This man welcomes sinners, and eats with them.'

Then Jesus told them this parable: 'Suppose one of you has a hundred sheep and loses one of them. Doesn't he leave the ninety-nine in the open country and go after the lost sheep until he finds it? And when he finds it, he joyfully puts it on his shoulders and goes home. Then he calls his friends and neighbours together and says, "Rejoice with me; I have found my lost sheep." I tell you that in the same way there will be more rejoicing in heaven over one sinner who repents than over ninety-nine righteous people who do not need to repent.

'Or suppose a woman has ten silver coins and loses one. Doesn't she light a lamp, sweep the house and search carefully until she finds it? And when she finds it, she calls her friends and neighbours together and says, "Rejoice with me; I have found my lost coin." In the same way, I tell you, there is rejoicing in the presence of the angels of God over one sinner who repents.'

Jesus continued: 'There was a man who had two sons. The younger one said to his father, "Father, give me my share of the estate." So he divided his property between them.

'Not long after that, the younger son got together all he had, set off for a distant country and there squandered his wealth in wild living. After he had spent everything, there was a severe famine in that whole country, and he began to be in need ...

'When he came to his senses, he said, "How many of my father's hired servants have food to spare, and here I am starving to death! I will set out and go back to my father and say to him: Father, I have sinned against heaven and against you. I am no longer worthy to be called your son; make me like one of your hired servants." So he got up and went to his father.

'But while he was still a long way off, his father saw him and was filled with compassion for him; he ran to his son, threw his arms round him and kissed him.

'The son said to him, "Father, I have sinned against heaven and against you. I am no longer worthy to be called your son."

'But the father said to his servants, "Quick! Bring the best robe and put it on him. Put a ring on his finger and sandals on his feet. Bring the fattened calf and kill it. Let's have a feast and celebrate. For this son of mine was dead and is alive again; he was lost and is found." So they began to celebrate.

'Meanwhile, the elder son was in the field. When he came near the house, he heard music and dancing. So he called one of the servants and asked him what was going on. "Your brother has come," he replied, "and your father has killed the fattened calf because he has him back safe and sound."

'The elder brother became angry and refused to go in. So his father went out and pleaded with him. But he answered his father, "Look! All these years I've been slaving for you and never disobeyed your orders. Yet you never gave me even a young goat so I could celebrate with my friends. But when this son of yours who has squandered your property with prostitutes comes home, you kill the fattened calf for him!"

'"My son," the father said, "you are always with me, and everything I have is yours. But we had to celebrate and be glad, because this brother of yours was dead and is alive again; he was lost and is found."'

The context (vv1–2) and the parable of the prodigal son (vv11–31)

The two groups in the opening verses represent two different responses to a strange temptation with which everyone must wrestle whenever they are presented with the Christian gospel. It is the temptation to try to earn God's love through our own efforts. The same two responses to this temptation are found in the parable of the prodigal son.

The Pharisees and the older brother represent those people who feel they are succeeding in their efforts to be the kind of person God might love. They have become proud and self-satisfied. Such people gravitate towards communities of 'people like us' and look down on those whose lives are not so pristine. Sadly some churches seem to have these characteristics. Ironically, such people don't much feel the need for the love of God they set out to earn in the first place. Instead, they bask contentedly in the approval of their peers.

The sinners and tax collectors and the prodigal son represent people who feel they are failing in their efforts to be the kind of person God might love. They have become increasingly uncomfortable in normal society. In Christian circles, people who are trying and failing to be deserving of God's love become self-conscious and might drift out of church into company they consider less demanding. Such people can't receive the love of God because they've tried and failed to earn it and don't believe they're worthy.

Neither group is particularly attractive but if you had to identify yourself with one of the groups which would it be?

- Are you more often tempted to pat yourself on the back, overly confident in your righteousness like the Pharisees and the older brother?
- If so, what are the dangers for your faith?
- How can you address pride and self-sufficiency?

- How can you recover the gratitude that should accompany our recognition of God's love and search for us?
- Or are you more often tempted to focus on your failings like the tax collectors and sinners and prodigals?
- Do you find it hard to believe God is seeking you because you feel dirty and embarrassed?
- If so, how can you be reassured of God's love?

You might be able to work through this yourself by reading and meditating on Scripture. But if there are particular past experiences or current struggles which make it difficult for you to accept God's love, you might consider talking and praying with a pastor or trusted, mature friend about these issues.

The parable of the lost sheep (vv3–7)
- Here the coming God is portrayed as a shepherd, what does that image mean to you?
- In what area of your life might you have strayed from the path and be in need of being carried home by a rejoicing shepherd?

The parable of the lost coin (vv8–10)
- Here the coming God is portrayed as an old woman; what does that image say to you?
- Does this image of God offer insights that might balance more common representations as King, Creator and Lord?
- The old woman is diligent in her search. She lights a lamp and sweeps through all the various spaces of her small house.

- Are there areas of your life where God is shining his light?
- Perhaps highlighting underused gifts that you might bring to his service?
- Perhaps identifying rubbish in your life that must be swept away so that the thing of value can be recovered?

PRAYER

Father, I thank You that You loved me and searched for me while I was still a sinner. Help me to continue to rejoice in Your love for me and to resist the temptation to rely on my own achievements. Amen.

CHAPTER 8

WHAT IF I'M NOT GOOD ENOUGH?

In the last chapter, we reflected on the 'coming God' who sets out to look for us. We saw that He does not wait for us to turn to Him or to clean up our lives. 'While we were yet sinners, Christ died for us' (Rom. 5:8, ESV). But what if we feel we're still not good enough, even after God has found and saved us? Woodbine Willie's answer to that question, as to so many others, was to point towards Jesus Christ. In Jesus Christ we see a measure of goodness which we could never hope to replicate. Fortunately, Jesus is not merely an example of goodness to be imitated. He is the author of goodness and he can empower us to live for Him. Woodbine Willie's message to us: You're not good enough, but Jesus is.

> What Jesus did for the men of His time, what He does for the men of all time, is to hold up before them a new order of goodness, a fresh motive of life. He bids them seek and find "Eternal Life," a phrase which never meant

to Him a kind of golden-harps-and-snow-white-wings-and-everlasting-hymns-before-the-great-white-throne existence, which was to come as a reward after death, but a new kind of life which was to begin here and now – at once. It was indeed never to find its completion and perfection in this world, but it was to begin here – begin in the honest and earnest search after that new order of goodness which Jesus showed to men as the goodness of God the Father.

If a man or a woman honestly accepts that challenge, and sets out upon the quest of the Holy Grail of Jesus' goodness, he will begin to understand why Christians are so definite and determined about Jesus Christ as being "His only begotten Son our Lord," "God of God, Light of Light, Very God of Very God," etcetera. He will become convinced that to talk of a Person who was the Author and actual Example of this sort of goodness as being just a "good man" is to use language without any real meaning. There never was a "man," however "good," who was like this. When you honestly start to live on this level, and stop arguing about it, you may come to the conclusion that Jesus' goodness is impossible, unpractical, visionary, mad, but you will not talk nonsense about its being "merely human." You may rail at it and Him as being inhuman and insane, and then His splendid wholesome sanity and His humanity in the best sense will stand up and ask you questions. He was a mad fanatic who played with children. He was a morbid puritan who declared war on natural instincts, and was called a glutton and wine-bibber and the friend of the harlots, who forgave the woman taken in adultery. He was a ridiculous visionary with His eyes fixed on Heaven who was always telling men that their first duty was to love one another and do good in this world. He was a megalomaniac madman who was always talking about Himself as King of Heaven, and always thinking about other people, and living the simplest and humblest life of kindly service. He made Himself equal with God, and forgave the men that spit on His face. He was a weak and womanish pacifist who would not strike an honest blow, who faced a Cross with the dignity of a hero, and died unbroken at the end. He was impossible, and infinitely appealing. If you set out to follow him in earnest, you may say in your heart that He is "the God of unutterable beauty Who breaks the hearts of men," but you will cease to use the cant of the critic who calls Him a very good man.[1]

Woodbine Willie lived through a period of history when radical forces sought to remake the world through class war and revolution. He was drawn by the power of such dreams because working men and women occupied a special place in his heart. In his youth, he had rallied working men to the revolutionary cause. He once shared with them the burning desire to take up arms, to overthrow the reigning powers and lift up the oppressed.

But Woodbine Willie was a realist about human nature. The duties of a parish priest had given him a window into the souls of men and women. He knew human weakness. He would not be fooled into thinking that the leaders of a revolution would, in the end, prove any better than the leaders they overthrew. He continually argued that what was needed was not revolution but transformation. The only hope for society was the regeneration of the human heart through encounter with Jesus Christ.

Continually, he held up Jesus Christ as the example of all that was best in humanity. He saw in Jesus a life so unique, so utterly unlike any other human biography that it appears as a series of impossible paradoxes – the driven fanatic with all the time in the world to bounce children upon his knee; the puritan known for loving nothing so much as a party; the otherworldly mystic with hands calloused from making His living as a carpenter; the man fully aware of His own greatness yet humble enough to wash the feet of common labourers. 'He was impossible, and infinitely appealing.'

But for Woodbine Willie, Jesus was never just a man. In fact, He was never less than God. This meant that to follow Him was never a question of willpower or determination or hard work. That kind of pull-yourself-up-by-the-bootlaces approach was as doomed to failure as the communist dream of revolution then utopia, and for the same reason. Human sinfulness and weakness make it impossible for us to imitate Christ by our own efforts.

Fortunately, we are not reliant on our own strength. In Woodbine Willie's words, Jesus is the 'author' as well as the 'example' of the kind of goodness His life exemplified. As 'author' of this goodness and, indeed, of all that exists, He is able to offer us a qualitatively new kind of life – eternal life. For Woodbine Willie the promise of eternal life is not some magic ticket to the hereafter, to a life after death that goes on and on and on (although it certainly includes that). Rather it is an infusion of life and power from Jesus to us right now. It is this infusion of goodness from the Author of goodness that makes it possible for us to begin to live the kind of life that He lived, the kind of life that can begin to build a new order of goodness into the world.

In another passage, Woodbine Willie emphasises that we can only receive this infusion through personal encounter with God in Jesus Christ:

> To attempt to worship a God without a name is to attempt the impossible. The universal can grip and hold us, but always, and only, through the particular. We may say that we worship Beauty; but it does not lay hold of us, thrill us, and transform us, until we see a beautiful thing, or know a beautiful person. We say we love Goodness; but goodness never really captures us until it looks at us with human eyes, speaks with a human voice, and is expressed in noble

deeds. We may follow the white star of Truth; but it is always the desire to know the truth of something, or of somebody, that stirs us to suffer and to sacrifice. "We fall in love with persons, not with qualities. It is just you, here and now, that we turn to, not to any abstract construction out of general principles." That is as true of God as it is of my Mother. Religion is falling in love with God; and it is impossible to fall in love with an abstract God, He must have a name ... The Christian faith says boldly to mankind, "Come, let us introduce you to God. His name is Jesus, and He was a Carpenter by trade. Hold out your hand, and He will take it in His. Shake hands – shake hands first – and then, because if you really see Him you will feel like that, kneel down."[2]

It is only on our knees before Jesus that we can receive this infusion of God's own eternal life and allow him to be 'good enough' on our behalf.

REFLECTION

All through Woodbine Willie's life and writings we find evidence that he considered the vision of Christ to be the beginning of a great venture for Christ. Salvation in Christ was to be the start not the end of the Christian journey. We are all called to a life of serving Christ through serving others. He was aware that this required the transformation of our fallen humanity, a transformation that Jesus Christ could offer because He was not just a good man but, rather, the good God. He was not just the example of the good life but the Author of the good life. In this time of reflection and application, we will consider Jesus as both example and Author.

Jesus as the example of the good life

READ PHILIPPIANS 2:1–11

Therefore if you have any encouragement from being united with Christ, if any comfort from his love, if any common sharing in the Spirit, if any tenderness and compassion, then make my joy complete by being like-minded, having the same love, being one in spirit and of one mind. Do nothing out of selfish ambition or vain conceit. Rather, in humility value others above yourselves, not looking to your own interests but each of you to the interests of the others.

In your relationships with one another, have the same mindset as Christ Jesus: who, being in very nature God, did not consider equality with God something to be used to his own advantage; rather, he made himself nothing by taking the very nature of a servant, being made in human likeness. And being found in appearance as a man, he humbled himself by becoming obedient to death – even death on a cross!

Therefore God exalted him to the highest place and gave him the name that is above every name, that at the name of Jesus every knee should bow, in heaven and on earth and under the earth, and every tongue acknowledge that Jesus Christ is Lord, to the glory of God the Father.

In this passage, the apostle Paul calls on his readers to imitate Christ's attitudes and replicate his willingness to lower Himself in order to serve others. By reflecting on the passage, by comparing ourselves to Jesus, we can begin to identify the areas where our own goodness needs to develop.

Which of the negative attitudes which are common to all human beings do you most struggle with?

- Are selfish ambitions directing your life, making your decisions for you? (v3)
- Are there areas of your life where you are tempted to be proud or conceited? (v3)
- Are you disadvantaging others because you constantly prioritise your own interests? (v4)

Which of the positive attitudes and behaviours exemplified by Christ would you most like to build into your life?

- Obedience? Do you need strength to respond to a challenge or a call God has given you?
- Humility? What distortions to your view of yourself can Christ clarify?
- Service? Are there people who need something you can offer – time, money, expertise?

Jesus as the author of the good life

READ JOHN 15:1-11

I am the true vine, and my Father is the gardener. He cuts off every branch in me that bears no fruit, while every branch that does bear fruit he prunes so that it will be even more fruitful. You are already clean because of the word I have spoken to you. Remain in me, as I also remain in you. No branch can bear fruit by itself; it must remain in the vine. Neither can you bear fruit unless you remain in me ...

As the Father has loved me, so have I loved you. Now remain in my love. If you keep my commands, you will remain in my love, just as I have kept my Father's commands and remain

*in his love. I have told you this so that my joy may be in you
and that your joy may be complete.*

An emphasis on Christ as the example of goodness can
become a heavy burden to bear if it is not balanced
by an emphasis on Christ as the Author of goodness
capable of infusing His life into us.

We have seen that Christianity is a movement from God
to us, an outpouring of His love and mercy. Even when we
come to Him, the power to live the Christian life is His
gift which we have only to receive. Because Christianity is
about grace, God's unmerited favour, it is always a mistake
to try to do things in our own strength.

We have just looked at Philippians 2 and considered
how our lives might fall short of God's desires for us.
We've considered actions we might take to address these
failings. But, still, we mustn't allow this process to become
a work of our will, or an act of our determination.
Instead, we must learn to receive strength by abiding in
Christ, allowing his life and power to flow through us.

**Consider, under what circumstances do you find it
easiest to experience God's presence? How can
you most easily receive the love and empowering of
Christ? For example:**

- Is it in church services surrounded by your brothers
  and sisters in Christ?
- Is it in private listening to worship music?
- Is it in prayerful walks in the countryside?
- Is it in periods of silence and mediation?
- Is it in receiving support and prayer from a
  Christian friend?

The way in which you encounter Christ doesn't matter. But if you are trying to follow the Philippians path of taking on the mind and the attitudes and the behaviours exemplified by Christ, you must make sure you also take time to abide in Him in prayer and worship (in whichever way works best for you) to receive His love and His joy. This is where the infusion of the eternal life of Christ will be received.

A short poem written by Woodbine Willie for his son reinforces this point:

TO CHRISTOPHER

Bear Thou the Christ,
My little son.
He will not burden Thee.
That Holy One.
For, by a mystery,
Who bearest Him He bears
Eternally,
Up to the radiant heights
Where angels be,
And heaven's crimson crown of lights
Flames round the crystal sea.[3]

PRAYER

Lord Jesus, help me to follow Your example, not through straining and striving, but through spending time in Your presence and absorbing Your life and strength. Amen.

CHAPTER 9

WHAT IS THE WORLD ALL ABOUT?

Sometimes it feels as if we are continually banging our heads against a brick wall, as if the world itself is resisting our attempts to build a good life. Sometimes the world seems to throw curveballs and play underhand tricks – sudden illness, unexpected unemployment, unforeseen relationship breakdown. Perhaps we shouldn't be surprised that a fallen world treats us this way. But Woodbine Willie argues that it is possible to see the true meaning of the world and to live without banging our heads against brick walls. Even a fallen world is God's world and it exists to serve His purposes. Our calling is to align our lives with the purpose of God revealed in Jesus Christ.

In the beginning was the Word – S. John i. 1.

There are no words that have ever been penned by the hand of mortal man which contain profounder wisdom than the opening verses of the Fourth Gospel. If I ask you ... to concentrate your thought upon the passage, it is not with any idea that we can together reach the hidden depths of its meaning, or exhaust its in-exhaustible treasures of Truth, but because no honest thought about it, after prayer for the light and guidance of the Holy Spirit, can fail to be fruitful of real results.

The opening phrase "in the beginning," carries our minds not merely back to the beginning of time, but beyond time and space altogether. It lifts us above things to the ultimate meaning and value of things. It would be better to translate it: "Right at the heart of ultimate reality," or "At the back of everything." The word "was" is also timeless, implying a mode of existence without beginning and without end, and we could best render it by the phrase: "Was in the beginning, is now, and ever shall be world without end," by which we strive to express eternity. The WORD, whether we take it as Greek or Hebrew in origin, cannot mean less than a Person expressing a rational purpose which I can, in some measure, understand. It is certainly Personal, and the idea of a Person who is "a word" must mean a person who expresses a rational idea or purpose in such a way that it can be understood by men. Thus if we translate the five Greek words as "Right at the heart of the ultimate reality there was in the beginning, is now, and ever shall be world without end, a Person expressing a rational purpose which men can in some measure understand," we get nearer to the meaning of the words ...

We do not claim to know God face to face, and in His fullness; but we do claim, and claim emphatically, that through Jesus Christ, we are growing in true knowledge of Him. We do claim that whatever new knowledge of God comes to us, either as a race or as individuals, whether it comes through science or through history, will never contradict Christ. In Christ the meaning of Life is being revealed. We only see things truly as we see them all in Him. His will and His purpose are the will and the purpose of all things, and only as we use all things in accordance with His will, and or His purpose, do we use them rightly. His purpose and not our purposes. His will and not our wills. That is the essential point. If we try to take the world and mould it to our wills, and make it conform to our purposes, it will break us in pieces. It will break our hearts, and burst our brains. The world is not yours – but God's; it is not made to serve your purpose but to serve the purpose of God revealed in Christ ...

Our supreme hypothesis is that in Christ we have revealed to us the ultimate nature of our environment, the true meaning, value and purpose of life.[1]

Human intelligence is very good at seeing patterns in random phenomena and creating meaning even where it doesn't exist. At one time or another we've all pointed to the sky to draw the attention of friends to the intricate shapes of animals or persons in the random patterns of the clouds. The internet is full of photos of slices of burnt toast in which people can see the face of Elvis Presley. Less amusingly, when walking alone in the dark every rustling leaf and cracking twig becomes evidence of an assailant creeping up behind us.

An atheist may view this last tendency to conjure meaning as merely an essential survival technique bequeathed on us by evolution. In an earlier phase of human development, when every rustling leaf and cracking twig really might have been a predator, such hypersensitivity increases your chances of survival. In the modern world, we are less susceptible to predation. But at the same time it has become clear that humans need meaning if we are to flourish. This presents a problem for the atheist whose universe is no more than a random collection of atoms that happen to have come together in the present into a remarkable pattern that includes human life and consciousness. Because, presumably, everything that has come together randomly will fall apart randomly, leaving nothing but cold, dark space. In such a universe the only meaning our lives can have is the meaning we create for ourselves. For atheists, meaning-making is still a survival technique. Now it protects us from the existential threat of meaninglessness rather than the physical threat of predators.

And so, men and women use their imagination and intellect to develop life-projects and so invest their existence with meaning. People can build life projects around almost anything – a career, a family, even a football team. This is where the world's curveballs and underhand tricks hit us. Meaning disintegrates when, perhaps through no fault of my own, my football team are relegated, my career hits the skids or my family breaks-up. Or, perhaps most perplexing of all, I achieve everything I've ever dreamed of and then discover I'm still not satisfied!

The tough and resilient pick themselves up and start all over again, redeveloping the same project with different personnel, or choosing another option entirely. Many people go through life hopping from project to project, continually meaning-making then continually disappointed. In other words, they are banging their heads against a brick wall.

In the passage we have just read, Woodbine Willie suggests that this continual frustration is the result of going against the grain of the world. 'If we try to take the world and mould it to our wills, and make it conform to our purposes, it will break us in pieces. It will break our hearts, and burst our brains.' If we want to avoid the experience of broken hearts and burst brains, Woodbine Willie tells us we must set aside the many different meanings imposed upon the world by human imagination and intellect and uncover its true meaning. He makes the remarkable statement: 'In Christ we have revealed to us the ultimate nature of our environment, the true meaning, value and purpose of life.'

This isn't the imposition of a layer of made-up meaning over the meaningless material universe. It is suggesting that the universe itself actually has its meaning in Christ. To use an old analogy, Jesus Christ is not like a sticker pasted on to the outside of the universe to change its appearance. He is actually written all through the very substance of the universe like the writing within a stick of seaside rock.

To live your life in imitation of Jesus Christ, in line with the teaching He gave while He lived on earth, and in the power of the Spirit He poured out on His followers, is to live life with the grain of the universe. To orient your life towards worshipping and serving Jesus Christ in order to play your part in bringing about His purposes in the world is to align yourself with the aim and goal of the whole universe. It is to live as human life was supposed to be lived on this planet.

This does not mean that our lives will be free of difficulty and pain. After all, it's a fallen world that we're called to begin to restore to its original good state. As a prophet of the suffering God, Woodbine Willie believed God's people were called to transform the world through their suffering as much as through their victories.

How does God deal with sin [and restore a fallen world]? By what way does He conquer? By the way of the Cross, the way of love. He suffers for it; He takes it upon Himself, and He calls on us to share His burden, to partake of His suffering. He makes an army of the Cross, an army of men and women who pledge themselves to fight with sin and gladly suffer in the fight, that by their strife and suffering the power of evil may be broken and the world redeemed.[2]

However, once we have had revealed to us what the world is all about, we will not be in danger of our life projects constantly being reduced to rubble by circumstances beyond our control. Our life project becomes Jesus Christ's life project which is destined to succeed, not necessarily today or tomorrow or even in our lifetime, but in God's time.

REFLECTION

We want to align our lives with the purposes of God and, therefore, to live our lives with the grain of the universe rather than banging our heads against a brick wall. We will consider how to achieve this re-alignment shortly, with reference to a wonderful passage of Scripture written by the apostle Paul to the Roman church. But, as a first step, it is essential we recognise Jesus Christ for who he truly is.

READ JOHN 1:1

In the beginning was the Word, and the Word was with God, and the Word was God.

Read and reflect on this verse and re-read the first two paragraphs of the quotation from Woodbine Willie that opened this chapter.

- Does Woodbine Willie's interpretation of this verse now make sense to you?
- Does it add to your understanding of what God was revealing to us about Jesus Christ through the Gospel writer, John?

John realised that Jesus Christ was not just a Jewish man walking and talking and healing His way through first-century Palestine. He understood that it was not even enough to see Jesus Christ as truly God, the risen Lord, standing at the side of the Father in heaven, ruling the universe by His command. We must see Jesus as the 'Word of God' written through the entire universe. He is the force and the logic at the centre of every quantum particle, hydrocarbon molecule, strand of DNA, human life, constellation of planets and every galaxy. All things have their beginning their living and their ending in Him and through Him (Col. 1:15–20).

READ ROMANS 8:18–39

I consider that our present sufferings are not worth comparing with the glory that will be revealed in us. For the creation waits in eager expectation for the children of God to be revealed. For the creation was subjected to frustration, not by its own choice, but by the will of the one who subjected it, in hope that the creation itself will be liberated from its bondage to decay and brought into the freedom and glory of the children of God.

We know that the whole creation has been groaning as in the pains of childbirth right up to the present time. Not only so, but we ourselves, who have the firstfruits of the Spirit, groan inwardly as we wait eagerly for our adoption to sonship, the redemption of our bodies. For in this hope we were saved. But hope that is seen is no hope at all. Who hopes for what they already have? But if we hope for what we do not yet have, we wait for it patiently.

In the same way, the Spirit helps us in our weakness. We do not know what we ought to pray for, but the Spirit himself intercedes for us through wordless groans. And he who searches our hearts knows the mind of the Spirit, because the Spirit intercedes for God's people in accordance with the will of God.

And we know that in all things God works for the good of those who love him, who have been called according to his purpose. For those God foreknew he also predestined to be conformed to the image of his Son, that he might be the firstborn among many brothers and sisters. And those he predestined, he also called; those he called, he also justified; those he justified, he also glorified.

What, then, shall we say in response to these things? If God is for us, who can be against us? He who did not spare his own Son, but gave him up for us all – how will he not also, along with him, graciously give us all things? Who will bring any charge against those whom God has chosen? It is God who justifies. Who then is the one who condemns? No one. Christ Jesus who died – more than that, who was raised to life – is at the right hand of God and is also interceding for us. Who shall separate us from the love of Christ? Shall trouble or hardship or persecution or famine or nakedness or danger or sword? As it is written:

'For your sake we face death all day long; we are considered as sheep to be slaughtered.'

No, in all these things we are more than conquerors through him who loved us. For I am convinced that neither death nor life, neither angels nor demons, neither the present nor the future, nor any powers, neither height nor depth, nor anything else in all creation, will be able to separate us from the love of God that is in Christ Jesus our Lord.

'The sufferings of this present time are not worth comparing with the glory that is to be revealed to us.' (vv18 and 20–2, ESV)

Aligning our lives with the purpose of God in Christ, and thus the true meaning of the world, is not a passport to an easy life. Suffering remains inevitable in a fallen world that is only on its way to being reconciled in Christ. His victory, though assured, is not yet absolute. Nonetheless, we must learn to discern between suffering which is a natural part of living and serving God in a fallen world, and suffering which is a result of our being out of alignment with God's plans and purposes for our lives:

- What are the areas of life or the circumstances which most often cause you suffering?
- Is the suffering simply the result of living in a fallen world? For example, suffering caused by unavoidable ill-health, watching the struggles of loved ones who will not accept help, undeserved unemployment or financial hardship?
- Or is at least some of the suffering due to you trying to make your own meaning, developing your own life project against the purposes of Christ and against the grain of the universe?
- For example, are you creating tension in your relationships by putting your dreams ahead of others' needs, or driving yourself into the ground pursuing the kind of standard of living the advertisers claim is needed but which is not really necessary?

'And we know that for those who love God all things work together for good, for those who are called according to his purpose.' (vv28 and 19–30, ESV) This passage reveals the purpose towards which the whole universe is oriented, 'the freedom of the glory of the children of God' (v21). This is what the world is all about. When we align ourselves with God's plan and purpose for the redemption of all of creation, we are going with the grain of the universe which was created by Christ and is shot through with Christ. Is this the hope that orients your life and gives you a purpose?

This passage also give us some clues as to how to re-align our lives in accordance with God's purposes revealed in Christ: 'The Spirit helps us in our weakness' (v26).

Here we see that the Spirit is at work in our lives, especially through prayer and intercession. This process often involves the Spirit revealing to us which parts of the life projects we imagine for ourselves are in God's plans and purposes for us and which are not. This process often includes the 'inward groaning' of frustrated plans and discarded dreams. Are there hopes and dreams which you need to let go because you know, deep down, that they are not part of God's plan for your life? Are there other hopes and dreams that you need to continue to wait for patiently (v25) because they are dreams given by God? Allow the Spirit into your heart and mind to sift these dreams and desires.

All of this is a joy rather than a burden because we know that nothing 'in all creation will be able to separate us from the love of God in Christ Jesus our Lord' (v39, ESV). It's not always easy to see how our insignificant lives can contribute to God's great purpose, the restoration of all things in Christ. In later chapters we will consider some of the ways Woodbine Willie understands even the most 'normal' of lives to be making a difference.

PRAYER

Spirit of God, come work in my life, help me to align my dreams and my plans with the purpose of God in Christ, and empower me to play my small part in the restoration of all things. Amen.

Part 4

VENTURE

TRANSFORMING THE WORLD

CHAPTER 10

WHAT IS THE CHURCH DOING HERE?

Since the very earliest days of the Christian faith, God's people have met together for worship, prayer, teaching and communion. We know that God is present and is pleased when His people gather together in His name. However, Church was never intended to be a club for the religiously minded. Woodbine Willie viewed the Church as one part military hospital and one part special-forces training camp! As far as he was concerned, joining the Church meant you were committed to the great venture of transforming the world.

Great heavens, how it rained, and just when we did not want it to rain! Fine dry weather just then would have saved many a British mother's son. It need not have rained either, it was not winter, it was the end of June, 1916. Fine weather would have been seasonable and reasonable, and this flood was neither, it was just cussedness.

We were preparing for the Great Offensive. I had just come up to the front as Chaplain to the Boys Brigade. I had never seen a trench and never heard a gun go off. I learned, from conversation with the men, that they were under orders that night to go up from billets to dig what they called a kick-off trench out in front of their present line. It was a rotten job at any time, they told me, and in this weather, it would be the rotten limit. There were generally casualties on these stunts.

What ought I to do? I had no orders. These men were my parish, anyhow. I must go where my parish goes. That was the line of argument I took with myself. I must go up ...

Fear came. There was a pain underneath my belt. Of course I had to go. It was the parish. We crept out. We could not go down into the two-foot ditch that they had made, it was crowded with men. We went along the edge. I whispered some inane remark as I passed by, and was rewarded all along the line with a grin which even darkness could not hide, and often, when I had passed, with the muttered comment, "Gaw blyme if it ain't the parson!" Vaguely I felt that this journey was worthwhile.

About a hundred and fifty yards along the trench we were brought to a halt. Two German flares shot up. We stood stock still. I felt that I must be visible to every Bosch in France, as I stood in that sudden silver world of light. They sailed right over us and then died out and left a deeper darkness over all.

"You'd better get into the trench, Padre," whispered the captain.

I was in it before he said it. I never moved so quickly in my life. There was silence for what seemed an age and must have been a minute. The men had ceased to dig. Then a hail of machine gun bullets burst over us with a noise like bitter hatred and foul words. A cry or a grunt here and there told me that some men were hit. Then it stopped, and I could hear nothing but a voice close by muttering, 'God! God! God!' through set teeth, with a swift hissing intake of breath between each word. Then like a sudden thunderstorm the shelling burst upon us. No, that is wrong; it was like no earthly thunderstorm. A thunderstorm is natural and kindly; it speaks of sultry summer days and ordinary things. If it speaks of wrath at all it is the wrath of Heaven, and through it comes a human voice; but this was the wrath of hell and hatred, the hatred, not of men, but of gigantic fiends. I can remember kneeling up to the waist in water watching the reflection of the bursting high explosives on the surface of it, saying the Lord's Prayer, and wondering about Death, the beauty and the silver reflections, fear, and bloody mothers' meetings. Presently I mastered the terror in my inside, and became more conscious of those around me. The man immediately in front of me had lost his nerve and was crying, and pleading with God for mercy. The man behind was better, he was swearing steadily at the Germans, and kicking me and saying between his oaths –

"Go on! Go on!"

"I can't go on," I shouted back; "the chap in front of me has got the hump or the blue jibbers or something."

A tremendous kick was the reply, and then in tones of puzzled fury –

"Who the hell's that?"

The situation was getting comic.

"This is the Church," I roared back.

Then came the great question.

"And what the %^&* is the Church doing here?"[1]

'What the %^&* is the Church doing here?' It is, as Woodbine Willie observes, a great question. I imagine he heard it many, many times through his life. As we have seen, he chose to serve alongside the frontline soldiers in the trenches. He frequented pubs and doss houses filled with disreputable drunks and tramps. He lived most of his life in the slum areas of industrial cities where ragged children ran riot. He stood alongside organised labour as they fought for better working conditions and pay. He seemed not to have much time for 'More tea, Vicar?' with the well-to-do.

Woodbine Willie took Jesus as his example. And the Gospels show us Jesus appearing in surprising places, engaging with the 'wrong' sorts of people, and acting in unexpected ways. He seemed to enjoy parties. He constantly broke taboos. He sat alone with a woman with a bad reputation and offered her the hope of a new life. He touched those who were considered unclean. He invited despised enemy collaborators to join His band of disciples. He announced that a Roman soldier had more faith than any of His own people. He caused mayhem in the Temple, the most sacred space on earth, by kicking over the money changers' tables. He ended up hanging on a cross between two criminals; everyone assumed He was cursed by God.

If we understand His mission correctly we find that these are not unexpected, wrong or surprising actions at all. Jesus did not think His mission was the formation of a nice club for the religious minded, certainly not the provision of family-friendly entertainment for the morally sensitive. He understood His ministry as a mission to the poor, the captive, the blind and the oppressed (Luke 4:17–21). He came to offer practical hope to those who were sick – spiritually, morally, socially and physically (Luke 5:31).

Increasingly, today we see Christians imitating Jesus as Woodbine Willie did. Like Woodbine Willie, they're expanding their understanding of 'the parish'. Heading out into no man's land, he told himself: 'These men were my parish, anyhow. I must go where my parish goes.' Today Christians are following the 'wrong' sorts of people into surprising places and they are serving this 'parish' in unexpected ways. For many, living for Christ is no longer a Sunday-only activity.

On a Saturday night in the centre of town you will find Street Pastors offering emotional support and practical help to young men and women who have made themselves vulnerable through excessive alcohol intake. All around the country, every morning of the working week, drop-in centres and kitchens run by Christians will open to provide newly arrived immigrants and asylum seekers a place to gather, eat and learn. Every night of the week, on street corners, in back alleys and in dingy corridors and cheap rooms, Christian support workers will offer friendship, a shoulder to cry on and the offer of a way out to sex workers. On estates all over the country, detached youth workers engage with gang members loitering in parks and alleyways and they bring them news of different and new opportunities.

But these are still the exceptions that prove the rule. Often these are the initiatives of specialist organisations and professionals. We've probably not yet come to the point we need to, where we see the Church's mission primarily as being 'out' there in the world. Most church members still think their primary Christian responsibility is to be in the pews on a Sunday morning, gathered together to sing a few songs and listen to a talk. There is a huge army of men and women which could be released into the world to bring the good news of Jesus Christ, in all its practical and spiritual power, to a broken world.

> The Church of Christ has, indeed, come to a point where she must choose and make up her mind as to whether she is going to accept or reject this gospel of the Kingdom. She must decide whether her purpose and duty is to rescue a certain number of individuals out of a lost and ruined world, and to bring them to such a pitch of personal piety that they will be safe from the world to come – or whether it is her purpose and duty to claim the whole world for Christ; to enter boldly into the world of commerce, industry, education, and politics, and declare that there, as everywhere else, His Will must be done, and He must be acknowledged King. It is a tremendous choice; and upon the way in which it is made, depends both the method and the message of salvation.[2]

This is Woodbine Willie's challenge to us. Will we go out into the world and answer the powerful question: *What on earth is the Church doing here?*

REFLECTION

In many ways, our Christian lives will be defined by how we answer these questions:

- What pleases God? Do we think that God is pleased only by our sung and spoken worship?
- Do we think God is pleased only by our keeping ourselves pure and uncontaminated by the sin in the world?
- Do we think God is pleased only by our religious practices of Bible reading, prayer and tithing?

- Or do we believe that God is also pleased when we take Christ out into the world to serve unlikely people in unusual ways and unexpected places?

Woodbine Willie often had Old Testament passages in mind when he wrote about the purpose and mission of the church. Indeed, he often quoted snatches of these passages from memory. Portions of the book of the prophet Isaiah appear to have been particular favourites.

READ ISAIAH 1:12–17

When you come to appear before me, who has asked this of you, this trampling of my courts? Stop bringing meaningless offerings! Your incense is detestable to me. New Moons, Sabbaths and convocations – I cannot bear your worthless assemblies. Your New Moon feasts and your appointed festivals I hate with all my being. They have become a burden to me; I am weary of bearing them. When you spread out your hands in prayer, I hide my eyes from you; even when you offer many prayers, I am not listening.

Your hands are full of blood!

Wash and make yourselves clean. Take your evil deeds out of my sight; stop doing wrong. Learn to do right; seek justice. Defend the oppressed. Take up the cause of the fatherless; plead the case of the widow.

This prophecy is given to the people of Judah and Jerusalem at the geographical and spiritual centre of God's activity. Yet God is less concerned by their religious observances and their worship than He is by the way they are living in the wider world.

Their prayers will not be heard until God's people cease to do harm to others; learn to do what is right; seek justice for all; bring hope to the orphans; and plead on behalf of the widow.

READ ISAIAH 58:6–12

Is not this the kind of fasting I have chosen to loose the chains of injustice and untie the cords of the yoke, to set the oppressed free and break every yoke? Is it not to share your food with the hungry and to provide the poor wanderer with shelter – when you see the naked, to clothe them, and not to turn away from your own flesh and blood? Then your light will break forth like the dawn, and your healing will quickly appear; then your righteousness will go before you, and the glory of the LORD will be your rear guard. Then you will call, and the LORD will answer; you will cry for help, and he will say: here am I.

If you do away with the yoke of oppression, with the pointing finger and malicious talk, and if you spend yourselves on behalf of the hungry and satisfy the needs of the oppressed, then your light will rise in the darkness, and your night will become like the noonday. The LORD will guide you always; he will satisfy your needs in a sun-scorched land and will strengthen your frame. You will be like a well-watered garden, like a spring whose waters never fail. Your people will rebuild the ancient ruins and will raise up the age-old foundations; you will be called Repairer of Broken Walls, Restorer of Streets with Dwellings.

Similarly in this passage, God tells His people that their fasting will not be considered valid until they share their food with the hungry; bring the homeless

into their own homes; clothe the naked; and pour themselves out for the afflicted. And lest we be tempted to think these are only Old Testament values, we should note that Jesus had something very similar to say when he was pressed on the question of what determines eternal destiny (Matt. 25:31–46).

In the following poem, Woodbine Willie watches a column of battle-weary and wounded British soldiers snaking down a road in France. In their ragged uniforms, their dirtiness and their physical brokenness, he sees something of exceptional beauty. The men reflect something of Jesus Christ who allowed himself to be torn to rags and broken beyond repair for the good of others.

If we are willing to leave the comfort of our buildings and go out into the world to serve unlikely people in unusual ways and unexpected places, we might well become a little ragged around the edges, a little bit broken, but I am sure God would see such a church as a thing of beauty.

SOLOMON IN ALL HIS GLORY

Still I see them coming, coming
In their ragged broken line,
Walking wounded in the sunlight,
Clothed in majesty divine.

For the fairest of the lilies,
That God's summer ever sees,
Ne'er was clothed in royal beauty
Such as decks the least of these.
Tattered, torn, and bloody khaki,
Gleams of white flesh in the sun,
Raiment worthy of their beauty
And the great things they have done.

Purple robes and snowy linen
Have for earthly kings sufficed,
But these bloody sweaty tatters
Were the robes of Jesus Christ.[3]

PRAYER

Father God, show me what pleases You and send me out into the world to serve You in the power of Your Spirit and to the glory of Your Son. Amen.

CHAPTER 11

WHAT IS THE POWER OF PRAYER?

Prayer is one of the great privileges of the Christian life – an invitation to relate one-to-one with the Creator of the Universe. However, it is also the source of some of our most perplexing problems. How do we reconcile the sweeping statements with which Jesus endorsed the power of prayer with our experiences of prayer unanswered? In the following text, one of his toughest pieces of writing, Woodbine Willie explores the true meaning and power of prayer. His starting point is what he perceives to be the cowardly, sinful prayer of a soldier crying out to God for protection while the shells crash down around him. Woodbine Willie uses this example to challenge us to confront the selfishness of much of our prayer. As usual, his real concern is to see the world changed to reflect the glory of Jesus Christ. He wants to encourage the kind of prayer that empowers us to play our part in the great venture of transforming the world.

In the trenches during a heavy bombardment. It lasted over two hours. We could do nothing but sit still and wait. A sergeant on one side of me swore great oaths and made jokes by turns. A man somewhere on the other side kept praying aloud, in a broken and despairing kind of way, shivering out piteous supplications to God for protection and safety.

I wish that chap would chuck that praying. It turns me sick. I'd much rather he swore like the sergeant. It's disgusting, somehow. It isn't religion, it's cowardice. It isn't prayer, it's wind. I'd like to shut him up. He probably seldom, if ever, prayed before, and now ho substitutes prayer for pluck, but it's all for safety. I hate this last resort kind of religion; it's blasphemy. The decent men all despise it. Look at the sergeant's face. The other chap keeps banging into his mind a connection between Christ and cowardice. That's where the blasphemy comes in. There is not, and there cannot be, any connection between Christ and cowardice ...

"Whatsoever you ask in My name, I will do it for you." It is a sweeping kind of promise, and easily misunderstood. Lots of Christians seem to think it means that prayer is a kind of magic cheque upon the bank of Heaven, only needing the formal endorsement with Christ's name to make it good for anything.

Of course it does not come off. Millions of such cheques are dishonoured every day. When the war broke out there was a regular run upon the bank of God, and our churches were thronged with distracted people waving cheques for protection, duly endorsed "through Jesus Christ our Lord," and still the German host swept on ...

Now what's this poor devil thinking about? Not his duty, not his pals; he's forgotten all about them. His whole mind is filled with one idea; the safety of his own skin. Well, don't be hard on him. Perhaps he has a wife and a kiddie at home, like your Patrick. I don't want to be hard, but I must be Christian. This is not prayer at all. Cowardice has turned it into sin. It is sin, not prayer. To think of one's own skin now, to pray for one's own safety, is sin. There is no such thing as selfish prayer.

There is no such thing as prayer which does not put God first ...

Prayer is the means of communication by which the suffering and triumphant God meets His band of volunteers and pours His Spirit into them, and sends them out to fight, to suffer, and to conquer in the end.

Prayer will not turn away the shell from my body; it will not change the flight of the bullet; but it will ensure that neither shell nor bullet can touch me, the real me. Prayer cannot save me from sorrow, but it can draw the sting of sorrow by saving me from sin. And in the end, through prayer and the army of those that pray, God will reach down to the roots of war and tear them from the world. When at last through prayer the stream of the Spirit has flowed out to all, men will look upon their guns their bombs, their gas cylinders as mad monstrosities, and will take the metal from the earth to mould and beat it, not into engines of death, but into means of beauty and life.

Prayer, true prayer, will bring us victory. For victory comes at last to those who are willing to make the greatest venture of faith, and the supremest sacrifice. By prayer we can reach Berlin. But more than that, by prayer we can conquer war itself, and march at last into the New Jerusalem of God.[1]

This is challenging stuff and probably strikes us as a little unfair. I think I see myself in that man pleading with God for his safety, perhaps you do too. I'm not sure I'm ready for the kind of tough-love pastoral care that Woodbine Willie practised. But Woodbine Willie is not really heartless. He later relents: 'I mustn't curse this poor beggar. He's just gone under. He's lost the spirit. I was nearly so bad, for I had nearly lost it too. I must not curse him. I must pray for him.' Then, typically: 'Probably I'd better begin with a fag. Have a fag, lad?' The essay finishes with the horror of a direct hit and explosion. Woodbine Willie has to be dug-out of the wreckage – 'That you there, sergeant? Well pull me out will you?' The 'coward's' prayers for safety have gone unanswered like so many before. 'This lad's dead. He never lit that fag.'[2]

We have all known seemingly unanswered prayer. As Woodbine Willie provocatively puts it: 'Millions of such cheques [drawn against the Bank of Heaven] are dishonoured every day'. There is no question but that the trenches would have undermined anyone's faith in the power of prayer:

From the soldier's point of view the condemnation of such prayers begins with the conviction, bought by bitter experience, that they do not work. Religion as an insurance policy against accident in the day of battle is discredited in the army. The men have lost what faith in it they ever had. Just as the rain descends upon the just and the unjust, so do the shells, and good and bad, praying and prayerless, are shattered into bits. It is terrible and as true as life. The flying death that shrieks in a shell is as impartial as an avalanche or a volcano.[3]

For Woodbine Willie the problem was not with prayer itself but with the *kinds* of prayers that were being prayed – self-interested prayers for personal protection. His model of true prayer is based upon the Garden of Gethsemane where Jesus Christ pours out His heart to God in the hours before His arrest and crucifixion.

To make his point, Woodbine Willie must divide the speech recorded in the Gospels into two parts. The first words of Christ, 'If it be possible let this cup pass from me' are, for Woodbine Willie, not a prayer at all, simply a natural expression of human terror. The true prayer is the second utterance: 'nevertheless, Thy will be done.' Here, says Woodbine Willie, we see prayer as it should be – prayer for the strength to do the will of God. As Jesus prays:

> Terror dies within His soul, hesitation disappears, and with His battle prayer upon His lips, "Thy will be done," He goes out from the garden in the majesty of manhood to bear such witness to His truth, to live in death so fine a life, that He becomes the light in darkness of every age, and the deathless hope of a dying world.[4]

There is value in Woodbine Willie's focus on prayer as the means by which God prepares us to go out into the world to do His will – to serve unlikely people in unusual ways and unexpected places. We will explore this further in the Reflection section below but, first, we must consider whether Woodbine Willie's understanding of prayer, as presented in the essay we are considering, is helpful.

We have observed that one of the most exciting characteristics of Woodbine Willie's thought is the fact that he was no ivory tower academic, painstakingly crafting theology from the comfort of an armchair. However, in this case it is possible to argue that the extreme conditions under which this essay was written have distorted his view of prayer.

In the trenches fear was inevitable and constant but panic could be contagious and often disastrous. Panic could all too easily result in the deaths of many men as discipline disintegrated and training was forgotten. We know from his writings that Woodbine Willie himself struggled with fear and frequently had to fight to keep his panic under control. In such particularly horrible circumstances, screaming out prayers for divine protection was precisely the sort of behaviour likely to spread panic and I think this is why Woodbine Willie considered such pleas to be selfish and almost blasphemous. But does that necessarily mean that the plea for protection itself cannot be seen as a natural and genuine expression of prayer?

If God is our Father, it seems natural and right that we would cry to Him for protection under such circumstances. It seems to me that this is the obvious understanding of Jesus' plea in Gethsemane that, if possible, the cup of suffering be allowed to pass from Him. It does not seem to me that Woodbine Willie is right to dismiss this as something less than genuine prayer. If we call God, Abba – Daddy – then we are bound to turn to Him with cries for help when life gets tough. I don't believe any human father would be offended by such a cry for protection and I do not believe God is offended when we call to Him in our fear.

However, prayers motivated by fear and selfishness, though understandable, may not be the kinds of prayers that God can answer in the way we would like. Prayer is not, as in Woodbine Willie's analogy, like a cheque on the Bank of Heaven that we can use to buy whatever we like – protection or prosperity or the spouse of our dreams, for example. Rather it is one of the means by which God's kingdom is gradually growing in the world.

This is why I think Woodbine Willie is right to see Jesus' second utterance in Gethsemane, 'nevertheless not my will but your will be done', as an expression of a far higher and truer prayer. The prayer with which we offer ourselves to God to be used in His service according to His will is the form of prayer towards which we should be growing. This 'is the means of communication by which the suffering and triumphant God meets His band of volunteers and pours His Spirit into them, and sends them out to fight, to suffer, and to conquer in the end.' This is the deeper more potent prayer which will empower God's people in their venture to transform the world for Christ.

REFLECTION

While Woodbine Willie does not solve the whole problem of unanswered prayer, he does provide us with one important piece to the puzzle. Sometimes the problem of unanswered prayer is actually the problem of selfish prayer. God is not offended by it. It is genuine prayer. But, in a broken world, it is not a prayer that always results in deliverance from trouble or the satisfaction of our wants. As with Jesus in Gethsemane, it may be that the only answer to this prayer is the comfort of knowing that God is with us, the promise of the courage to endure, the faith to say, 'nevertheless, not my will but Thy will be done', and the hope that in the end we will be with God in a place where all sorrow and mourning, fear and pain have been replaced by joy and celebration.

Woodbine Willie understood the problem of selfish prayer to be the fault of the religious teachers:

We have taught our people to use prayer too much as a means of comfort. Not in the original and heroic sense of uplifting, inspiring, strengthening, but in the more modern and baser sense of soothing sorrow, dulling pain, and drying tears. The comfort of the cushion, not the comfort of the cross.[5]

If this was true in Woodbine Willie's day, I imagine it is much more the case now. Some of us may have been encouraged to view our religion like any other lifestyle option. Too often, we are invited to judge churches on the basis of what they offer, as if they were health clubs. Too often, we have been taught a prosperity gospel in which God's favour can be cashed in for material wealth. Too often, we have been offered a therapeutic account of faith as simply the means to emotional and psychological wholeness.

Our understanding of the purpose of prayer is inevitably influenced by this cultural setting and we will do well to listen closely to Woodbine Willie's challenge and interrogate our own prayer lives, alert for signs that we are stuck in a self-interested form of prayer. If we do find such signs, the best approach is to try to replace me-centred prayers with other-focused prayers. We can take time to consider the needs of those around us and pray for strength and wisdom to play our (possibly small) part in showing God's love to them. Rather than praying for our own comfort we can ask to be empowered and guided in comforting others.

READ PAUL'S PRAYERS – ROMANS 15:30–33; PHILIPPIANS 1:19–21; EPHESIANS 3:14–21

In the New Testament letters written by Paul to different churches, we are given an insight into his understanding and practice of prayer. As we look now at some examples, we will see that he was not averse to praying, and asking for prayer, for personal protection. However, it is clear that he was far more interested in the furthering of God's purposes than in his own physical wellbeing.

And we will see that the greater part of his prayer resembles the kind Woodbine Willie celebrated, prayers for transformation and empowering for mission and ministry in the strength of the Holy Spirit.

As you read the following passages, compare Paul's prayers and his comments on prayer with your own prayer life. Consider how much time you spend on different kinds of prayer. Consider whether you could say 'Amen' to Paul's prayers and statements. Reflect on whether you could imagine yourself saying and praying these words:

Praying for protection: Romans 15:30–33

I urge you, brothers and sisters, by our Lord Jesus Christ and by the love of the Spirit, to join me in my struggle by praying to God for me. Pray that I may be kept safe from the unbelievers in Judea and that the contribution I take to Jerusalem may be favourably received by the Lord's people there, so that I may come to you with joy, by God's will, and in your company be refreshed. The God of peace be with you all. Amen.

Praying for God's will no matter the personal cost: Philippians 1:19–21

for I know that through your prayers and God's provision of the Spirit of Jesus Christ what has happened to me will turn out for my deliverance. I eagerly expect and hope that I will in no way be ashamed, but will have sufficient courage so that now as always Christ will be exalted in my body, whether by life or by death. For to me, to live is Christ and to die is gain.

Prayer for empowering for mission and ministry: Ephesians 3:14–21

For this reason I kneel before the Father, from whom every family in heaven and on earth derives its name. I pray that out of his glorious riches he may strengthen you with power through his Spirit in your inner being, so that Christ may dwell in your hearts through faith. And I pray that you, being rooted and established in love, may have power, together with all the Lord's holy people, to grasp how wide and long and high and deep is the love of Christ, and to know this love that surpasses knowledge – that you may be filled to the measure of all the fullness of God.

Now to him who is able to do immeasurably more than all we ask or imagine, according to his power that is at work within us, to him be glory in the church and in Christ Jesus throughout all generations, for ever and ever! Amen.

PRAYER

Abba Father, I know that You love me and care for me; help me to grow in prayer until I am less concerned with my own comfort and more concerned with how I can bring comfort to others. Amen.

CHAPTER 12

WHAT CAN
WE DO ABOUT
SUFFERING?

Suffering is an unavoidable component of human experience in this broken world. Whether suffering is thrust upon us by events in our own lives, or by our sensitivity to the suffering of others, we will one day be called to face its challenge. Woodbine Willie knew about suffering. With his first-hand knowledge of ill-health and war, and a lifelong commitment to the poor and marginalised, he was well placed to reflect upon this issue. He recognised that those who follow Jesus Christ and venture all to serve Him, must know how to engage with suffering.

On June 7th, 1917, I was running to our lines half mad with fright, though running in the right direction, thank God, through what had been once a wooded copse. It was being heavily shelled. As I ran I stumbled and fell over something. I stopped to see what it was. It was an undersized, underfed German boy, with a wound in his stomach and a hole in his head. I remember muttering, "You poor little devil, what had you got to do with it? Not much great blonde Prussian about you." Then there came light. It may have been pure imagination, but that does not mean that it was not also reality, for what is called imagination is often the road to reality. It seemed to me that the boy disappeared and in his place there lay the Christ upon His Cross, and He cried, "Inasmuch as ye have done it unto the least of these my little ones ye have done it unto me." From that moment on I never saw a battlefield as anything but a Crucifix. From that moment on I have never seen the world as anything but a Crucifix. I see the Cross set up in every slum, in every filthy overcrowded quarter, in every vulgar flaring street that speaks of luxury and waste of life. I see Him staring up at me from the pages of the newspaper that tells of a tortured, lost, bewildered world.

"Ever and always I can see set up above this world of ours, a huge and towering cross with great arms stretched out from East to West, from the rising to the setting sun, and on that Cross my God still hangs and calls on all brave men and women to come out, and share His sorrow and help to save the World" ...

But the Vision of Life in the Cross is not a vision of despair, but of confidence and hope, because behind it there is the empty tomb, and the figure with wounded hands outstretched to bless, ascending into glory. That completes the WORD made Flesh which reveals the meaning of Life. Without that we would go mad ...

We must die to live, and we can never do it except through the Power of His Resurrection. It is the Risen and Ascended Christ that saves. The fourfold picture is one in Truth. A new Birth without a Crucifixion is impossible, a Crucifixion without a Resurrection would drive any human being stark staring mad. He would commit suicide, which is the maddest of all mad things, an attempt to murder God. To see the world as a Crucifix without an empty tomb would be a vision too terrible for any human being to look upon, it would drive him, like Judas, shrieking with horror into the night to which there are no stars. We must have the whole faith. The meaning of Life is Advent, Christmas, Good Friday, Easter Day, Ascensiontide, and Pentecost – for the Word became Flesh and dwelt amongst us – and that was the manner of His dwelling.[1]

Earlier in the book from which this quotation is taken, *The Word and the Work*, Woodbine Willie tells the sad story of an old woman he knew during his time in France. One day he came across her after a heavy bombardment. She was 'sitting on the roadside near to her two cows which had been literally torn to pieces, wiping her wounded face, and crying through her tears: "Le bon Dieu, il est mort! Le bon Dieu, il est mort!" ("The good God's dead.")'[2]

All around Woodbine Willie were men who were echoing the old lady's cry. In the trenches, amidst the suffering of soldiers, civilians and animals, it was easy to conclude the good God was dead. In the face of those who thought Christianity was meaningless and worthless, Woodbine Willie offered a response to suffering that is neither naïve nor hopeless. In chapter 3, The Thought of Woodbine Willie, we considered his theology, now we will look at the practical application of that theology.

First, Woodbine Willie was convinced that Christians must be willing to look suffering full in the face. In the passage above, he stops to see the suffering in all its horror: 'As I ran I stumbled and fell over something. I stopped to see what it was. It was an undersized, underfed German boy, with a wound in his stomach and a hole in his head.' Woodbine Willie had a particularly soft heart. In fact, he considered a hardened heart to be evidence of a cowardice worse than any cowardice in battle. His anger burned against those who dared to offer trite and simplistic religious answers to the problem of suffering. Therefore before we can even begin to do something about suffering, we must recognise its reality and its challenge to us. It cannot be ignored or wished away or dismissed with platitudes.

Second, when we look suffering full in the face, we can be assured that God understands and is present with us. In Woodbine Willie's spark of imagination or revelation: 'It seemed to me that the boy disappeared and in his place there lay the Christ upon His Cross, and he cried, "Inasmuch as ye have done it unto the least of these my little ones ye have done it unto me."' Woodbine Willie's radical contention was that even today God does not merely look down on suffering from the luxury of heaven but continues to suffer with us. Whether or not we think this is the best way to understand the action of God in the world, we can be confident that in the event of the cross God has entered at least once into the very depth of human suffering. He knows what it is like.

This is a great gift which Christianity offers to the world which is not replicated in other religions or philosophies. The willingness of God to drink the cup of human experience to the very dregs, equips Him to be present with us in suffering in a way that no other human (let alone any other god!) could possibly replicate. When we cry out to God for strength in the midst of our own suffering, or when we cry out to God on behalf of others who suffer, our prayers do not have to travel the inconceivable distance from our broken world to the perfect glory of heaven. Rather we pray to One who is in the midst of the suffering, present by His Spirit. A Christian response to suffering knows that God is close to those who are suffering, not far removed on a heavenly throne or impervious to the pain of humanity.

Third, Woodbine Willie makes it plain that it is not enough for a Christian to preach the suffering of God. We must also preach the victory of God seen in the resurrection. Only by belief in a resurrected Lord, can we hope for an end to suffering and a restoration of all things: 'The Vision of Life in the Cross is not a vision of despair, but of confidence and hope, because behind it there is the empty tomb, and the figure with wounded hands outstretched to bless, ascending into glory.'

In 1 Corinthians 15, Paul makes a similar point:

> But if it is preached that Christ has been raised from the dead, how can some of you say that there is no resurrection of the dead? If there is no resurrection of the dead, then not even Christ has been raised. And if Christ has not been raised, our preaching is useless and so is your faith ... If only for this life we have hope in Christ, we are of all people most to be pitied.

We might paraphrase that last verse to say, if in Christ we have only the comfort of His having experienced suffering, we have little to celebrate. If, however, we remember that the crucifixion is only one part of the story, then hope remains.

Finally, in the power of the ascended Lord who has poured out His Spirit on us, we must work to relieve suffering and, eventually, eliminate suffering from the world. We must never allow ourselves to be comforters alone. It is not even enough to be preachers of hope to come in the future, we must commit ourselves to bringing hope *now*. We are called to strain every sinew to remove every instance of suffering from the world, rooting it out wherever we find it. Where there is poverty we must do what we can to bring relief. Where there is physical suffering we must both pray for healing and draw upon the remarkable advances in medicine that have occurred over recent years.

The Christian faith does not overlook suffering or treat it as an embarrassment to be swept under the carpet. The Christian faith recognises the terrible reality of suffering and points to the fact that our God knows first-hand what such suffering is like. We also argue that suffering is not the end of the story. Jesus Christ who suffered rejection by His friends, humiliation at the hands of His enemies, physical torture, a criminal's death and separation from His Father, also conquered suffering. His Spirit creates a community that is stronger than rejection, releases into the world the promise of a glory that negates humiliation, a healing that will restore all that is physically broken, a life that is stronger than death, and the promise of eternal reconciliation with the Father for all who call on His name.

REFLECTION

We will use the book of Job as an opportunity to reflect on good and bad examples of responding to the suffering of others.

Job is one of the most remarkable books in the Bible and yet we know very little about its origins or the exact question it was intended to address. Nonetheless, it is acknowledged (even by the non-religious) as one of the most beautiful and profound meditations on suffering which has ever been written. The narrative presents the terrible suffering of a once prosperous man. We readers are in on an important secret from the start. We know that Job's misfortune has nothing to do with anything he has done. There is no foolishness or unrighteousness on his part that leads to his suffering. When Job maintains his innocence throughout the book, we know that he is right to do so.

READ JOB 2:11–13

When Job's three friends, Eliphaz the Temanite, Bildad the Shuhite and Zophar the Naamathite, heard about all the troubles that had come upon him, they set out from their homes and met together by agreement to go and sympathise with him and comfort him. When they saw him from a distance, they could hardly recognise him; they began to weep aloud, and they tore their robes and sprinkled dust on their heads. Then they sat on the ground with him for seven days and seven nights. No one said a word to him, because they saw how great his suffering was.

The main human characters are Job, obviously, and his 'friends'. When they are first introduced into the story in these verses they behave in a way that, I believe, Woodbine Willie would consider exemplary:

- What can we learn from Job's friends' response to his terrible suffering?
- Is this a good example of being willing to look suffering full in the face? Why?
- What are the most common responses when people encounter suffering today?
- What might a response like the response of the 'friends' look like in our encounters with suffering friends and loved ones?

Sadly, the three friends do not continue to respond to Job's suffering in a helpful way. The 'friends' or 'comforters' are later revealed as self-satisfied, religious experts. Confident that their theology is correct, they offer exactly the kinds of trite explanations of suffering that Woodbine Willie would find disgusting. The friends insist Job admit his sin and repent. For example, here are the points at which each friend speaks for the first time:

- Eliphaz argues in 4:7–9 that the righteous do not suffer because God is just.
- Bildad argues in 8:1–7 that God cannot pervert justice by allowing a righteous man to suffer.
- Zophar argues in 11:13–20 that if only Job would repent, God will forgive and restore him.

They make their confident accusation on the grounds of a 'pet theory'! Their theology states that here and now, in this life on earth, the righteous will always prosper under God's blessing, and the unrighteous will always be punished by God. (You only have to read Psalms and Proverbs to see that this was a commonly held and orthodox piece of theology.) However, in this particular instance, we know they are wrong.

In fact, at the end of the book, God upholds Job and rebukes the three friends (Job 42:7–9).

After the LORD *had said these things to Job, he said to Eliphaz the Temanite, 'I am angry with you and your two friends, because you have not spoken the truth about me, as my servant Job has. So now take seven bulls and seven rams and go to my servant Job and sacrifice a burnt offering for yourselves. My servant Job will pray for you, and I will accept his prayer and not deal with you according to your folly. You have not spoken the truth about me, as my servant Job has.' So Eliphaz the Temanite, Bildad the Shuhite and Zophar the Naamathite did what the Lord told them; and the* LORD *accepted Job's prayer.*

As a result, we will do well to ask ourselves:

- What are my 'pet theories' about the causes of suffering?
- In what ways might I be using these to justify myself or insulate myself from the difficulty of facing up to undeserved suffering in the world?
- Might Jesus need to correct my view as he corrected the view that suffering was due to sin in an individual's or a parent's life (John 9:1–3)?

Do you think that there are times when any attempted explanation of the suffering and evil in the world can only have a negative effect upon those who are actually suffering? If so, think about what might such times be and what might we be able to do instead of trying to offer an explanation.

PRAYER

Father, make me a good friend to those who are suffering, sensitive to their questions and struggles but always mindful of the hope that we have in You. Amen.

CHAPTER 13

WHAT SHOULD I DO WITH MY MONEY?

Perhaps nothing is more challenging to Christians living in our consumer culture than working out how we should use our money. This challenge was of great importance to Woodbine Willie who grew up in an impoverished parish, chose to minister to the poor and gave his final years to the Industrial Christian Fellowship, encouraging workers in their pursuit of a future where there would be plenty for all. In his book *The Wicket Gate*, Woodbine Willie wrestles with appropriate and inappropriate attitudes to money. His unexpected answer to the question: *what should I do with my money?* Spend it on those you love!

> If any man says to me that he has no love of money, I immediately begin to wonder if he is a madman, a millionaire, or a tramp, those being the only types of people I can imagine saying it with anything like sincerity. You see, money gets mixed up with everything.

I may say that I do not love money; but I do love my son. I love him almost more than anything else on earth, and I desire for him the best that can be got. I desire for his mind the finest development of which it is capable. I desire for his body the best that fresh air, good feeding, and good housing can make of it; and I love to see him – as I have seen him within the last year – with his golden hair streaming in the wind, his blue eyes shining, and his brown legs twinkling, as he runs and shouts upon the shore beside a summer sea. I desire all these things for him, passionately desire them; and before God and my conscience, I cannot feel the desire is wrong, that it goes beyond what God meant to be daily bread. But I cannot get any of those things for nothing; I have to pay, and often pay through the nose.

So the love of money gets all mixed up with the love of children, the highest with the lowest; the best and worst within us meet, and seem confused ...

I may say that I do not love money; but I do love beauty, my hunger for it is, at times, like pain – and I can satisfy that hunger, and feast on the glory of God's world, finding not seldom in it a joy beyond my powers to express.

God give me speech, in mercy touch my lips,
    I cannot bear Thy Beauty and be still,
Watching the red-gold majesty that tips
    The crest of yonder hill,
And out to sea smites on the sails of ships ...

I remember sitting down to write that, as the sun went down behind the hills, and turned the sea into a mirror, that reflected all the glory wherein the great High Priest of Nature decks himself when he offers up the evening sacrifice. But as I drank in the beauty, I was conscious of bitterness in it, because even there I could not shut my ears to the cry of the City of Destruction. There were so many thousands and thousands of my fellow creatures who had every bit as much right to this as I had, and could not have it because they could not pay. Not merely because they could not pay the price of an exit from their prison of mean streets; but because the mean streets, had got into their souls and blinded their eyes, so that they could not have seen the beauty even had they been there. And there are thousands, thank God, who are beginning to experience this bitterness booause of othoro' wants ...

I cannot believe that God holds out the cup of this life's beauty to us, brimming over with its rich red wine, merely so that we may exercise our souls by refusing to put it to our lips. I believe that we were meant to drink, but I believe too that the cup of Beauty was meant to be a loving-cup. There is a sort of blasphemy about drinking it alone, like a solitary communion, that turns its beauty into bitterness. I want to share it with my fellows.

And so the problem of money gets all bound up with problem of love, and cannot be separated from it.[1]

This is an original response to the 'problem' of how we followers of Jesus Christ are to determine what we should do with our money. Woodbine Willie's approach has a balance that is often lacking in teaching on this subject. It is also unusually positive. It is built around the assumption God intends us to appreciate and enjoy the life he has given us rather than on rejection of the world. It is also about growing in virtue rather than eliminating perceived vices.

In short, the genius of the response is its focus on *love* rather than money.

We are used to being warned off love of money. It is a familiar refrain for preachers and it is good advice. But Woodbine Willie is astute enough to realise that, more often than not, sermons denouncing the love of money are preaching to the already converted. He understood that few of us really love money itself. But if we don't love money itself, why are we not more Christ-like in our relations with money? Why do we struggle to develop appropriate Christian disciplines in this area? Why do we still find it so hard to give a reasonable proportion of it away? Why is there still avoidable poverty and disease in the world? Woodbine Willie understands why; it is because 'money gets mixed up with everything'.

For example, money gets mixed up with our love of our children. We want the very best for them and the best costs. Any teaching that requires us to somehow downgrade our love of our children and our desire for the very best for them is unlikely to be applied. The desire to provide the best for our children is, I believe, not just a powerful desire but actually a God-given motivation.

Similarly, Woodbine Willie recognises that our love of money gets mixed up with our love of the world God has made. We want to enjoy to the full the world into which he has placed us. We want to travel out of the cities. We want to see natural beauty. We want to be refreshed by engaging with the natural world on our holidays and our days off. We want to taste the best of the fruit of the earth in food and drink. I am sure this is a God-given desire, an aspect of the 'wonder' that can actually lead us towards God. 'I cannot believe that God holds out the cup of this life's beauty to us, brimming over with its rich red wine, merely that we may exercise our souls by refusing to put it to our lips,' writes Woodbine Willie. To deny this desire to experience the best of the world can often lead to unhealthy super-spirituality, and turn us into people who are so heavenly minded that they are actually no earthly good.

Woodbine Willie realises that the only thing that will really change us is not less love but *more* love as he put it in the penultimate paragraph of the passage we have just read.

There is no point counselling parents to stop loving their children. What is needed is a new infusion of the Holy Spirit to cause more love to spring up for more of the children of the world. We are called to love not just our own children but our children's friends, and their peers in the poorer parts of town, and their generation all around the world. Especially, we are called to love those children growing up in conditions of poverty beyond our comprehension.

As it is with love of children, so it is with love of nature. Too often Christians have tried to discipline their attitude to money by denigrating the importance of the natural, material world. The results of this dismissal of creation look like being catastrophic. We begin to treat the world as a resource at our disposal, a tool to be used and then discarded. The environmental crisis which now threatens future generations is, at least in part, the fault of Christians who forgot what it meant to inhabit and love a world created by God and declared good.

We will know we are growing in this love when we are 'beginning to experience bitterness because of others' wants'. It is growing in love that will make us willing to work towards a more just and more beautiful world. Only when we have expanded the category of those we love to include many, many more of our brothers and sisters around the world will we be willing to pay something of the cost of transforming the world.

In short, what should we do with our money? Spend it on those we love!

REFLECTION

Getting to grips with the way we use our money is a complex process involving not just prayer and Bible study but also careful budgeting of income and outgoings, consideration of where our giving can be put to best effect, and building habits of simplicity and generosity over time. Here we will simply consider three passages from Matthew's Gospel that might help us to reflect further on Woodbine Willie's unusual approach of spending our money on those we love.

READ MATTHEW 7:9–12

Which of you, if your son asks for bread, will give him a stone? Or if he asks for a fish, will give him a snake? If you, then, though you are evil, know how to give good gifts to your children, how much more will your Father in heaven give good gifts to those who ask him! So in everything, do to others what you would have them do to you, for this sums up the Law and the Prophets.

Here Jesus builds His teaching on recognition of the natural human desire to want the best for our children. But there are then two moves to expand the arena of our natural generosity:

1. We see that God's desire to give good gifts extends to the whole human race;
2. We are challenged to act towards others in the ways we would have them act towards us.

We can begin to consider the implications of this passage for our lives by reflecting on the following questions:

- To whom do your feelings of natural generosity extend – immediate family, friends, children of the world, people in crisis, or the 'deserving' poor?
- Who remains outside of the scope of your natural generosity?
- Do you think God wants good things for them too? To which other groups might God want you to open your heart (and your wallet)?
- How would you like to be treated if you found yourself in great financial need?
- How might you begin to treat others in need to reflect the way you would like to be treated?

READ MATTHEW 22:37–40

Jesus replied: "'Love the Lord your God with all your heart and with all your soul and with all your mind." This is the first and greatest commandment. And the second is like it: "Love your neighbour as yourself." All the Law and the Prophets hang on these two commandments.'

Note that the two commands in this short passage do not exist in two separate, water-tight compartments. There is a link between the two. Indeed, it is impossible to love the Lord your God with all your heart without also beginning to love your neighbour. Your neighbour is also a child of your heavenly Father. Woodbine Willie believes that the only way to learn to use our money appropriately is to expand the breadth and the depth of our love.

- Who do you consider to be your neighbour?

- Which do you find harder, loving God or loving your neighbour?
- How do you express your love for God? How do you express your love for your neighbour?
- How do you think you can grow in your love for God and your love for your neighbour?

READ MATTHEW 25:31–46

When the Son of Man comes in his glory, and all the angels with him, he will sit on his glorious throne. All the nations will be gathered before him, and he will separate the people one from another as a shepherd separates the sheep from the goats. He will put the sheep on his right and the goats on his left.

Then the King will say to those on his right, 'Come, you who are blessed by my Father; take your inheritance, the kingdom prepared for you since the creation of the world. For I was hungry and you gave me something to eat, I was thirsty and you gave me something to drink, I was a stranger and you invited me in, I needed clothes and you clothed me, I was ill and you looked after me, I was in prison and you came to visit me.'

Then the righteous will answer him, 'Lord, when did we see you hungry and feed you, or thirsty and give you something to drink? When did we see you a stranger and invite you in, or needing clothes and clothe you? When did we see you ill or in prison and go to visit you?'

The King will reply, 'Truly I tell you, whatever you did for one of the least of these brothers and sisters of mine, you did for me.'

Then he will say to those on his left, 'Depart from me, you who are cursed, into the eternal fire prepared for the devil and his angels. For I was hungry and you gave me nothing to eat, I was thirsty and you gave me nothing to drink, I was a stranger and you did not invite me in, I needed clothes and you did not clothe me, I was ill and in prison and you did not look after me.'

They also will answer, 'Lord, when did we see you hungry or thirsty or a stranger or needing clothes or ill or in prison, and did not help you?'

He will reply, 'Truly I tell you, whatever you did not do for one of the least of these, you did not do for me.'

Then they will go away to eternal punishment, but the righteous to eternal life.

This challenging passage draws our attention to two important facts about the way we use our material resources, including our money. First, God is deadly serious about our using our material resources to alleviate the suffering of strangers, not just our immediate family. This is a matter of eternal consequence. Second, we see that it is not the quantity that is given but the quality of life out of which it is given that matters. The righteous did not give hugely valuable services or goods – a cup of water, a visit to a prisoner, some unwanted clothes but the fact that they had eyes to see the need and hearts open to playing their part is commended by God. You cannot grow to love or come to serve those that you can't even see.

- Are your eyes open to the suffering and need in the world around you, or are you so caught up in your own business that you might be missing the Lord hidden among the 'least of these'?
- What are the actions that you can take right now, regardless of the state of your own finances, which might be the equivalent of offering a cup of water or a visit to a prisoner?

PRAYER

Lord God, as I learn to love You may I also learn to love others, especially those who are suffering, and as I love help me also to give out of the resources You have given to me. Amen.

CHAPTER 14

WHAT IS THE SECRET OF GOOD SEX AND LOVE?

Flick through a magazine or turn on the TV and you will find news of another celebrity couple who have just divorced. People are asking whether partnership-for-life should be discarded as a throwback to our distant past, unsuitable for today's long life-spans and ever evolving careers. Simultaneously, the media rage around the question of sex without any hint of a consistent answer. Is society over sexualised or still too repressed? Should prostitution be legalised or more vigorously prosecuted? Do 'no strings attached hook ups' harm us or not? Although he was best known as a preacher and prophet, Woodbine Willie was also a pastor. Through years of chaplaincy, parish ministry and travel, he often thought, preached and wrote about sex and relationships. The following extract is taken from a series of lectures delivered to the officers and men of the British Army stationed on the Western Front.

[Sex] is God's provision for the act of union between men and women: it was meant to be an act which brought the whole man into play, body, mind and spirit, all made one in love. The act of intercourse was meant to be the crown of womanhood complete. It was meant to be our highest purely human joy, and where there is true love, it is.

Where a man and his own woman are made one flesh in love, there is no grander or more joyous thing than this fusion of their bodies and souls, through which a human soul takes flesh and men behold the glory of a child. This act which is at once the channel of creative power, and the crowning point of love, the glorious completion of an honest lover's kiss, is a thing of perfect joy and beauty forever in the world.

All true mirth and merriment, all solemn and sacred joy, all the best romance and chivalry surround it. It has been the soul of Music and the heart of Poetry ever since the world began. The bridal night of lovers that are loyal, that is human nature. The harlot in the brothel is just common human sin – the sin for which the Son of God came down to save the world.

O men, I am no cold, white-livered, passion-hating saint. I have loved, and I love now with all my body and my soul. I love a woman's beauty as the fairest thing on earth; it is not because that beauty is bad that I would keep it veiled, but because it is the sweetest and most sacred of God's gifts.

It is not because my passion is bad that I would keep it down, but because it is the best of me, the grandest gift I have to give, a gift I will not waste. I dare not blaspheme my God by using what was given me to make new life as an instrument of murder. Yes, murder. It is just solid, sober fact. The average life of a prostitute who has made it a regular profession is from three to five years.

Prostitution, as a traffic, is just slow murder, and not so very slow at that ... We cry out against our enemies as murderers of women and children, but we are not clean ourselves. The very hands that hold the sword of vengeance are stained with women's blood.

That is just the sober truth. It is better to rip a woman open and leave her disembowelled in the mud than to drive her into deadly sickness, to satisfy a self-created craving that we are too weak to fight ...

You rouse your passion and then you submit. Why buy post-cards of naked women and keep them, and show them round? Why use continually the word for intercourse that makes your passion hot? Why talk about the traffic as an everlasting joke? Why a dead set at a man who wants to keep his body clean? Why talk smut, think smut, and feed your soul on smut?

Come off it, I say. If you were half as full of nature as a strong man ought to be you would leave these things alone, because you would know that you couldn't touch them and be clean. A man whose manhood is unwasted knows the strength of passion, and he keeps it well in hand; he has no use for artificial stimulants. You create an atmosphere of smut and dirt, and then when you have made yourselves uneasy, you submit.

You fill your minds with thoughts of it, and then because by nature's law your body makes response, you blame the

God who made your bodies, not the lust which damns your souls. I say the necessity is an artificial one, which you can destroy if you will get together and fight.[1]

Surely, if any group deserved a 'get out of jail free' card for sexual morality, it would be men on the cusp of battle, unsure whether they would live or die. Many would choose to turn a blind eye to their attitude of 'eat, drink and be merry for tomorrow we die', but not Woodbine Willie. He preached against prostitution on the Western Front for the same reasons he later decried promiscuity and infidelity back in England. He believed these practices stood in the way of good sex and love. Promiscuity and infidelity were not natural and inevitable but sinful and damaging.

For example, Woodbine Willie's dislike of prostitution was not puritanical or ideological. It was because it was so destructive. His words equating the use of prostitutes with murder might seem over dramatic until you hear him tell how in pastoral ministry he frequently came across women who had worked on the streets and in the brothels. For example:

A woman in a common lodging house who was dying of pneumonia. She lay there half uncovered on a dirty bed ... and she kept muttering, "God damn all men, God damn all men, and curse their bloody bodies," and she died like that while I prayed.[2]

He believed that sexual promiscuity also damaged the men who he saw as the hope of Britain. He dreamed that after the war they would go home to build a better society. He did not want them to bring back 'stained bodies and stained souls [but] a manhood kept untarnished by the Power of the Christ.'[3]

So far, so conventional. You'd scarcely hold the front page for a clergyman condemning prostitution and promiscuity. The more radical aspects of Woodbine Willie's understanding of sex and love may be seen in three further points:

First, Woodbine Willie denied outright that the problems of sex could be blamed on God or nature. He argued that whether the problem is physical lust leading soldiers to the brothels, or a dreamy romanticism leading their wives back home into affairs, the seeds are sown by bad habits developed long before any damaging actions are taken. The soldiers spent a long time looking at 'smut' before they were driven to the brothel. Their wives filled their minds with sentimental romances long before they were tempted to act upon their day-dreams and let another man sweep them off their feet. According to Woodbine Willie, the Christian has a responsibility to resist temptation by refusing to get drawn into these harmful habits, not simply to excuse himself or herself with a shrug and an argument about what's natural.

Second, Woodbine Willie argued that *contra* fairy stories, romantic comedy, and the common sense of our culture, true love is the result of the commitment found in marriage rather than the other way around:

> Love is the result of monogamy and not its cause – that is the great fact upon which we must lay firm hold if we want to think sanely on sex and its significance in human life. Loyalty, tenderness, mutual consideration, sacrifice, and all that goes to make up the complex sentiment which we call love is ... the result of an increasingly successful attempt at monogamy which has been made down the ages and the tradition arising out of that attempt.[4]

Ideally, we go into marriage with strong feelings of attraction and affection and the beginnings of real love. But only within the zone of safety provided by life-long commitment can a man and a woman grow together and be joined at every level until something truly worthy of the name 'love' grows. When it is fully developed it is 'a thing of perfect joy and beauty'.

Third, Woodbine Willie was honest about how hard it is to live for Christ and follow His teaching on relationships. In his only novel, *I Pronounce Them*, he explores the meaning of sex and love through the interlocking stories of four different couples. He chose fiction because he could think of no other way to convey the 'agony' of trying to obey Scriptural teaching and develop committed relationships in a broken world. He considered the book 'a tale told by a fool striving to help his fellow fools, and guide their sorely wounded feet into the Way of Peace.'[5] The narrative is far from a traditional romance and none of the couples enjoy a conventional 'happy ever after'. Instead, the novel traces the long-term consequences of choices and actions, observing the devastation that ensues when men and women choose selfishly, either in the insatiable search for a perfect Mr or Miss Right or when driven by physical lust into infidelity and promiscuity.

At the end of the day, Woodbine Willie doubted there was any one 'secret' to good sex and love. But he was convinced that the teaching of Christ in Scripture was the only guide worth following. He also believed that only in Christ was there healing and hope for the many who had been damaged in these areas, often through no fault of their own.

REFLECTION

While there may be no one 'secret' to great sex and fulfilling relationships, there are certain attitudes and behaviours that will always keep us from enjoying the best of sex and love, for example, unbridled lust or dreamy romanticism. According to Woodbine Willie: we must address these problems at their roots, we must address these problems together, and we must address these problems by focusing on Christ.

Addressing the problems at their roots:
In many ways Woodbine Willie's teaching echoes the teaching of the book of James.

READ JAMES 1:13–18
When tempted, no one should say, 'God is tempting me.' For God cannot be tempted by evil, nor does he tempt anyone; but each person is tempted when they are dragged away by their own evil desire and enticed. Then, after desire has conceived, it gives birth to sin; and sin, when it is full-grown, gives birth to death.

Don't be deceived, my dear brothers and sisters. Every good and perfect gift is from above, coming down from the Father of the heavenly lights, who does not change like shifting shadows. He chose to give us birth through the word of truth, that we might be a kind of firstfruits of all he created.

Are you tempted to blame God for giving you too strong a sex drive or for putting a longing in your heart for romance your spouse can't or won't offer? Might it be that, a few steps back, you began making decisions that fed that sex drive or fed that frustrated romanticism? Are there habits of thinking, reading or looking that you need to cut out of your life to help you resist and remove temptation?

Addressing the problems together:
Woodbine Willie appreciated that this was not a battle which could be won alone. While private prayer and repentance, for example, are important, we also need the support of our Christian brothers and sisters.

READ EPHESIANS 4:1–16

As a prisoner for the Lord, then, I urge you to live a life worthy of the calling you have received. Be completely humble and gentle; be patient, bearing with one another in love. Make every effort to keep the unity of the Spirit through the bond of peace. There is one body and one Spirit, just as you were called to one hope when you were called; one Lord, one faith, one baptism; one God and Father of all, who is over all and through all and in all.

But to each one of us grace has been given as Christ apportioned it. This is why it says:

'When he ascended on high, he took many captives and gave gifts to his people.'

(What does 'he ascended' mean except that he also descended to the lower, earthly regions? He who descended is the very one who ascended higher than all the heavens, in order to fill the whole universe.) So Christ himself gave the apostles, the prophets, the evangelists, the pastors and teachers, to equip his people for works of service, so that the body of Christ may be built up until we all reach unity in the faith and in the knowledge of the Son of God and become mature, attaining to the whole measure of the fullness of Christ.

Then we will no longer be infants, tossed back and forth by the waves, and blown here and there by every wind of teaching and by the cunning and craftiness of people in their deceitful scheming. Instead, speaking the truth in love, we will grow to become in every respect the mature body of him who is the head, that is, Christ. From him the whole body, joined and held together by every supporting ligament, grows and builds itself up in love, as each part does its work.

Patience, humility and gentleness are also going to be important in this area.

- How can we demonstrate these qualities in supporting one another? (v2)
- What different parts might those with the gifts of 'pastors' and 'teachers' have to play in helping the community in this area? (v11)
- Do you think you need explicit permission/ invitation before 'speaking the truth in love' to a Christian brother or sister? Why or why not? (v15)
- What kind of work can we best do through each of the following – deep friendship, prayer/accountability groups, cell/home groups, congregations?
- What does 'maturity' look like in the context of good sex and love? Surely it doesn't mean you are never tempted or that your marriage is perfect! (v13)

Addressing the problems by focusing on Christ:

As discussed in an earlier chapter, Woodbine Willie saw Jesus Christ as the Author (as well as the example) of goodness:

Christ is your true leader ... You only find a brothel a necessity for your bodies because you fail to see that Christ is a necessity for your souls. You've got the whole thing twisted. Lust is a necessity, Christ a luxury, you say. It is the other way. Christ is a necessity, and lust a rotten luxury. No man has the honest right to say that lust is a necessity until he has tried Christ and found Him fail.[6]

READ PHILIPPIANS 3:8–11

What is more, I consider everything a loss because of the surpassing worth of knowing Christ Jesus my Lord, for whose sake I have lost all things. I consider them garbage, that I may gain Christ and be found in him, not having a righteousness of my own that comes from the law, but that which is through faith in Christ – the righteousness that comes from God on the basis of faith. I want to know Christ – yes, to know the power of his resurrection and participation in his sufferings, becoming like him in his death, and so, somehow, attaining to the resurrection from the dead.

We cannot win in this area through self-discipline or strength of will alone. We need God's help and, in particular, we need the righteousness that comes from God through faith in Christ (v9).

It is important to recognise that through no fault of their own, some people never find or enjoy good sex and love. Others find and enjoy it for a time and then have it taken away. Many men and women are left lonely and frustrated by bereavement, by divorce or simply because they never find a compatible partner. Woodbine Willie believed that it is only in the 'surpassing worth of knowing Christ Jesus' that those who suffer in this area could find hope, strength or restoration.

PRAYER

Father God, I know you want the best for me in every area of life. In my relationships help me to live for Christ and, whatever my circumstances, to please You in all that I think and say and do. Amen.

CHAPTER 15

WHAT IS THE POINT OF WORK?

Recently, a friend in 'secular' employment told me how frustrating it was that churches find time in their in services to pray for people called to a new ministry position (locally or in foreign missions) yet rarely, if ever, find time to pray for those who have been offered a position of responsibility in the workplace. A very high percentage of us spend vastly more of our time in work than in church activities. Learning to value our labour as done unto God, and in the service of God and his world, can transform our discipleship and all of our lives.

THE FAITH AND THE HOPE

When through the whirl of wheels and engines humming,
Patient in power for the sons of men,
Peals like a trumpet promise of His coming,
Who in the clouds is pledged to come again.

When through the night the furnace fires flaring,
Loud with their tongues of flame like spurting blood,
Speak to the heart of love alive and daring,
Sing of the boundless energy of God;

When in the depths the patient miner striving,
Feels in his arms the vigour of the Lord,
Strikes for a kingdom and the king's arriving,
Holding his pick more splendid than the sword.

When on the sweat of labour and its sorrow,
Toiling in twilight, flickering and dim,
Flames out the sunshine of the great to-morrow,

When all the world looks up – because of Him.
Then will He come – with meekness for His glory,
God in a workman's jacket as before,
Living again the Eternal Gospel Story,
Sweeping the shavings from His workshop floor.[1]

I want the miner to feel when he is down there in his pit that he is not merely working for his wage – working for Friday night – a wage slave, but that he is a priest of God, a priest of Love called by God to produce warmth and power for his brothers in the world. I want him to feel that he is as much a priest down there in the dark, filthy black and streaming with sweat, as I am a priest when I stand at the altar and plead for the wants of man. The coal black is as white as my white robes, and sweat is sacramental wine poured in service of God's world. He is the Right Honourable the Collier, one of the greatest and worthiest servants of the human race. I want him to feel that about himself, and I want other people to feel that about him. That's the Spirit, and that's the call that has in it power to destroy this dirty, muddled, ugly world, and build a city of God upon the ruins.[2]

Woodbine Willie completely rejected the idea of a sacred/secular divide. In his book, *The Wicket Gate,* he told of his consternation upon discovering Sunday School materials that taught that Sunday is 'God's day', the Bible is 'God's book' and the church is 'God's house'. Without wishing to deny the importance of the Sabbath, the Bible and the church, Woodbine Willie responded:

There is nothing in all the world except what is evil, which has not God's name written upon it. All things are His, and all things must therefore be used carefully and only for the right purpose. All days are His days, all books are His books, all houses are His houses. If our finding of God in the Churches leads to our losing Him in factories, it were better to tear the Churches down, for He must hate the sight of them. If we seek our God in the Sanctuary, and pass Him by in the street, it were better to break up the altars.[3]

He was also a passionate champion of working women and men. He believed they were the hope of the nation. His book, *Democracy and the Dog Collar,* opened: 'To the Working Men of Britain, Who were her soldiers once, this book is dedicated with affection and respect'. Because he loved the labourers, because he believed that

God was Lord of all, and because he believed that everything existed for God's glory, Woodbine Willie was certain that our work was important to God.

The poem we have just read is one of Woodbine Willie's more obscure efforts and, perhaps, requires re-reading before its meaning emerges. It is clear that the final verses tell of the second coming of Jesus Christ in the clouds in glory. But even 'Then will He come with meekness for His glory, God in a workman's jacket as before'. This is quite a remarkable suggestion. Woodbine Willie has such a high view of work that he thinks that even after the second coming Jesus will be a labourer, as he was for the first thirty years of his life as a builder/carpenter in Nazareth. Even when the Kingdom comes, even when the whole universe bows the knee and confesses that Jesus Christ is Lord, they will be confessing the Lordship of a worker, still willing to stoop and be seen 'sweeping the shavings from His workshop floor'.

It's a radical vision – so unusual as to seem strange, irreverent even. But, surely, it is not impossible. If all that we've been saying in previous chapters is true: if there is no sacred/secular divide; if God is as concerned with the material world as he is with the spiritual; if the kind of religion that pleases him is the practical religion that feeds the hungry, clothes the naked and houses the homeless, then why shouldn't the King of Glory spend some of eternity in a carpenter's workshop? After all at the end of the Gospel of John, we see the risen Lord cooking breakfast on the beach for his disciples (John 21:9–12)!

How might that radical vision transform our Monday to Friday lives? On this account, all work that is worthy of the name and is done in service of others, has eternal value. It is one of the ways in which God's kingdom is being built and the world is being transformed – ugliness into beauty, privation into plenty. No wonder Woodbine Willie sees the miner as 'the Right Honourable the Collier, one of the greatest and worthiest servants of the human race.' And also recognises that 'The Doctor, the Pioneer, the Scientist, are workers with God like the Priest. All good work is God's work, and all good workers do God's will. They are labouring to make a world."[4]

Practical men and women – manufacturers, plumbers, medics, farmers, pharmacists, educators, software engineers, rubbish collectors – are doing the work of the Lord because they are serving the needs of those that God loves. There is no sacred/secular divide because, as Woodbine Willie realised, in the beginning and at the end practical science and religion are one:

> "Our Father" is the beginning and the end of science, as it is the beginning and the end of life, for the beginning of science is the supposition that tho world is in reality a rational world, and the end of science is to understand, and so hold communion with that rational reality. The beginning of life is the supposition that God is Love, and the end of life is to comprehend, with all the Saints, what is the length, and breadth, and depth, and height, of that Love which passes knowledge. So science and religion meet and in the end are one.[5]

Creative men and women – designers, artists, writers, architects, builders, chefs – are doing the work of the Lord because they are bringing beauty into the world that God loves. Woodbine Willie believed that the vision of Jesus Christ and the inspiration of the Holy Spirit lay behind the greatest examples of human creativity:

> The glory of God in the Face of Jesus Christ ... in a thousand different forms, in passionate poetry, majestic music, in a blaze of perfect colour, in mysteries of arch and aisle, in splendour of white steeples, and strength of massive towers, the cry has been echoed down the ages – thine is the glory for ever and ever, Amen. It is in Bach's Mass in B Minor. It is in the spire of Salisbury and the towers of York.

Words fail me. What more can I say. Just the steady, sober
Truth of my own soul lost in the dark without Him.[6]

All our work is done unto Jesus Christ. He understands the
frustrations of our working lives. He might not have been bored
by endless data entry or hurt by water-cooler gossip but we can
suppose He too has sweated and probably been cheated, bashed
His thumb and torn His nail down to the quick. He understands
the value of our work because He has wielded tools and fought
with recalcitrant materials to address practical needs and to
bring more beauty into the world.

REFLECTION

It is possible that Woodbine Willie's position seems
fanciful and overstated to you. Could God really value
work as much as he suggests? To help us reflect on that
question, we will begin by looking at some Bible passages
that take us from the very beginning of the story to its
final conclusion and go some way towards uncovering
God's view of work. We will finish by taking the time to
read and meditate on a short poem by Woodbine Willie.

Read Genesis 2:1–17. Who engages in 'work' in this
passage? Do these verses come before or after the 'fall'
of humanity and the world? What do your answers to
these first two questions, taken together, say to you
about God's view of work, as understood from this
Genesis passage?

Even apostles don't get out of manual labour. In Acts
18:3 Paul stays with tentmakers Aquila and Priscilla in
Corinth and works alongside them as he shares the same
trade. Writing to the Corinthians some years later, he

notes that although as an apostle he could have claimed material reward for this spiritual labours, he never did so, preferring to earn his own keep (1 Cor. 9:14–18).

You might like to consider what these other New Testament passages suggest about God's views on the value and purpose of work: Ephesians 4:28; Colossians 3:22–4; 1 Thessalonians 5:13–18; and 2 Thessalonians 3:11–13.

READ REVELATION 22:1–5

Then the angel showed me the river of the water of life, as clear as crystal, flowing from the throne of God and of the Lamb down the middle of the great street of the city. On each side of the river stood the tree of life, bearing twelve crops of fruit, yielding its fruit every month. And the leaves of the tree are for the healing of the nations. No longer will there be any curse. The throne of God and of the Lamb will be in the city, and his servants will serve him. They will see his face, and his name will be on their foreheads. There will be no more night. They will not need the light of a lamp or the light of the sun, for the Lord God will give them light. And they will reign for ever and ever.

At the very end of the story, in the glory and splendour of the renewed heavens and earth, God's people continue to be referred to as his 'servants' (v3). They seem to have ongoing work to do, especially the 'healing of the nations', and they are called to 'reign' (v5).

Meditating on Woodbine Willie's poetry

Read the short poem and ask yourself the questions that follow:

WORK

Close by the careless worker's side,
Still patient stands
The Carpenter of Nazareth,
With pierced hands
Outstretched to plead unceasingly,
His Love's demands.

Longing to pick the hammer up
And strike a blow,
Longing to feel His plane swing out,
Steady and slow,
The fragrant shavings falling down,
Silent as snow.

Because this is my Work, O Lord,
It must be Thine,
Because it is a human task
It is divine.
Take me, and brand me with Thy Cross,
Thy slave's proud sign.[7]

What activity would the Lord find me engaged in if he came and stood close by my side at work?

- Would I feel embarrassed or proud to have him standing there watching me?
- Would my embarrassment or pride be due to the actual activity or the manner in which he would find me doing that activity?

What about my work might the Lord long to pick up and take part in?

- Are there aspects of my work which I value which would not interest Jesus?
- Are there aspects of my work which I undervalue but which Jesus might itch to get involved in?

What challenge does the final verse present to you?

- How might you work differently if you viewed your work as God's work?
- How might you work differently if you were branded with a cross to remind you in every moment that, ultimately, you are working for God's glory?

PRAYER

Lord Jesus Christ, help me to value work as You value it and always to conduct myself in a way that will please You and bring about Your purposes in the world. Amen.

CONCLUSION

The life and writings of Woodbine Willie have been a challenge and an encouragement to me for many years. I hope that in the pages of this book you have glimpsed something of what this remarkable man continues to offer to those of us trying to live for Christ in the twenty-first century.

I hope that in reading and reflecting you might have drawn some strength from Woodbine Willie's courage in the face of great suffering and in the face of the hardest questions that life in this fallen world can present to people of faith. In this life, final, definitive, satisfactory answers will probably continue to elude us as they eluded him, but with him we can trust ourselves to the God who loved us, sought us, found us and holds a glorious future ready for us.

I hope that in reading and reflecting you might have been challenged by Woodbine Willie's vision of the Christian life as a journey. We are called onwards from the first glimmerings of wonder, to a vision of God revealed in Jesus Christ and into the great venture of remaking the world to His glory. On that journey we experience the strength of Christ flowing through us in our working, our giving, our loving, our praying and our serving.

Above all, I hope that in reading and reflecting you might have been inspired by Woodbine Willie's passion for Jesus Christ. In Woodbine Willie's writings I find myself confronted afresh by the glory of God revealed in the face of Jesus Christ and I hope the same has been true for you. I can't imagine anything that would have made Woodbine Willie happier than the knowledge that many decades after his death his prose and poetry were still drawing people to Jesus Christ – the Lord he knew and loved even amidst the horrors of no man's land, the Lord he knows and loves now as he worships in His presence in glory.

FURTHER READING

All of Woodbine Willie's writings are out-of-print but if you are interested in reading more of his work, many of the titles you will find in the bibliography can be discovered online in facsimile versions or may be ordered through specialist second-hand book suppliers.

This book has focused on Woodbine Willie's wisdom but if you are particularly interested in Woodbine Willie's life, there are some excellent biographical resources available:

- Bob Holman, *Woodbine Willie: An Unsung Hero of World War One* (Oxford: Lion Hudson, 2013).

This excellent biography was my primary resource for the chapter on the life of Woodbine Willie. Bob Holman is an experienced biographer and offers a thorough and thoughtful account. Holman is best known as the 'good man of Glasgow', having spent a large portion of his life intentionally living alongside and serving some of the most deprived communities in Britain. This background gives him an immense sympathy for Woodbine Willie's passion for the poor and his commitment for serving them through parish ministry.

If you are willing to search out hard-to-find and out-of-print titles, there are other fascinating books available:

- Michael Grundy, *A Fiery Glow in the Darkness: Woodbine Willie, Padre & Poet* (Worcester: Osborne, 1997).

Michael Grundy is a local journalist on the Worcester Evening News. As a journalist, Grundy's writing style is extremely accessible and this short book also contains more photos and illustrations than other biographies.

- J. K. Mozley, ed., *G. A. Studdert Kennedy: By His Friends* (London: Hodder & Stoughton, 1929).

Published within months of Woodbine Willie's death, this is a moving account from those who knew him best, while they were still coming to terms with his loss and trying to assess the impact and importance of his life and ministry.

- William Purcell, *Woodbine Willie: A Biography* (London: Hodder & Stoughton, 1962).

For a long time, this was the definitive biography, described in the extended subtitle as: 'Being some account of the life and times of Geoffrey Anketell Studdert Kennedy poet, prophet, seeker after truth, 1883–1929.'

BIBLIOGRAPHY

Grundy, Michael, *A Fiery Glow in the Darkness: Woodbine Willie, Padre & Poet* (Worcester: Osborne, 1997).

Holman, Bob, *Woodbine Willie: An Unsung Hero of World War One* (Oxford: Lion Hudson, 2013).

Mozley, John Kenneth, ed., *G. A. Studdert Kennedy: By His Friends* (London: Hodder & Stoughton, 1929).

Purcell, William, *Woodbine Willie: A Biography* (London: Hodder & Stoughton, 1962).

Studdert Kennedy, Geoffrey Anketell, *Rough Talks by a Padre* (London: Hodder & Stoughton, 1918).

Studdert Kennedy, *The Hardest Part* (London: Hodder & Stoughton, 1918).

Studdert Kennedy, *Lies!* (London: Hodder & Stoughton, 1919).

Studdert Kennedy, *Democracy and the Dog Collar* (London: Hodder & Stoughton, 1921).

Studdert Kennedy, *Food for the Fed Up* (London: Hodder & Stoughton, 1921).

Studdert Kennedy, *The Wicket Gate* (London: Hodder & Stoughton, 1923).

Studdert Kennedy, *The Word and the Work* (London: Longmans, 1926).

Studdert Kennedy, *I Pronounce Them* (New York: George H. Doran, 1927).

Studdert Kennedy, *The Warrior, the Woman and the Christ* (London: Wyman & Sons, 1928).

Studdert Kennedy, *The New Man in Christ* (London: Hodder & Stoughton, 1932).

Studdert Kennedy, *The Unutterable Beauty* (London: Hodder & Stoughton, 1947).

ENDNOTES

Introduction: Running Into No Man's Land

[1]Studdert Kennedy, *Lies!* (London: Hodder & Stoughton, 1919), pp109–110.

[2]From *The London Gazette*, quoted in Bob Holman, *Woodbine Willie: An Unsung Hero of World War One* (Oxford: Lion, 2013), p63.

1. Why Woodbine Willie?

[1]Studdert Kennedy, *The Unutterable Beauty* (London: Hodder & Stoughton, 1947), pp135–40.

[2]Studdert Kennedy, Geoffrey Anketell, *Rough Talks by a Padre* (London: Hodder & Stoughton, 1918), p20.

[3]Holman, *Woodbine Willie*, p67.

[4]*Ibid*, p65.

[5]Studdert Kennedy, *The Unutterable Beauty*, p11.

[6]Studdert Kennedy, *Lies!*, p13.

[7]The original version of this brilliant observation is usually attributed to Oliver Wendell Holmes.

[8]Studdert Kennedy, *The Warrior, the Woman and the Christ* (London: Wyman & Sons, 1928), p25.

[9]*Ibid*, p16.

2. The Life of Woodbine Willie

[1]Holman, *Woodbine Willie*, p10.

[2]*Ibid*, p11.

[3]John Kenneth Mozley, *G. A. Studdert Kennedy: By His Friends* (London: Hodder & Stoughton, 1929), p17.

[4]Mozley, *By His Friends*, p39.

[5]Holman, *Woodbine Willie*, p16.

[6]*Ibid*, pp60–61.

[7]Holman, *Woodbine Willie*, p28.

[8]Mozley, *By His Friends*, pp61–62.

[9]*Ibid*, pp82–83.

[10]Quoted in Michael Grundy, *A Fiery Glow in the Darkness: Woodbine Willie, Padre & Poet* (Worcester: Osborne, 1997), pp38–39.

[11]William Purcell, *Woodbine Willie: A Biography* (London: Hodder & Stoughton, 1962), p115.

[12]Studdert Kennedy, *The Hardest Part* (London: Hodder & Stoughton, 1918), p49.

[13]Holman, *Woodbine Willie*, p36.

[14]Studdert Kennedy, *The Hardest Part*, pp112–113.

[15]Grundy, *A Fiery Glow in the Darkness*, p66.

[16]*Ibid*, p58.

[17]Holman, *Woodbine Willie*, pp89–90.

[18]*Ibid*, pp94–95.

[19]Purcell, *Woodbine Willie*, p10.

[20]Both quoted in Holman, *Woodbine Willie*, pp143–145.

[21]Mozley, *By His Friends*, pp63–64.

3.   The Thought of Woodbine Willie

[1]Studdert Kennedy, *Lies!*, p68.

[2]*Ibid*, pp78–79.

[3]Studdert Kennedy, *The Hardest Part*, p7.

[4]*Ibid*, p193.

[5]Mozley, *By His Friends*, pp59–60.

[6]Studdert Kennedy, *The Warrior, the Woman and the Christ*, p21.

[7]Studdert Kennedy, *The Hardest Part*, ppix–x.

[8]*Ibid*, p191.

[9]*Ibid*, p31.

[10]*Ibid*, pp34–35.

[11]*Ibid*, p47.

[12]*Ibid*, p10.

[13]Studdert Kennedy, *The Unutterable Beauty*, pp30–31.

[14]Studdert Kennedy, *The Hardest Part*, p44.

[15]*Ibid*, pp29–30.

[16]*Ibid*, p203.

4.   The Wisdom of Woodbine Willie: Finding the meaning of life in a journey of Wonder, Vision and Venture

[1]Studdert Kennedy, *The New Man in Christ* (London: Hodder & Stoughton, 1932), pp214–215.

5.   What is the Nature of Nature?

[1]Studdert Kennedy, *The Hardest Part*, pp15–19.

[2]Studdert Kennedy, *The Unutterable Beauty*, pp84–85.

6.   What is the Purpose of Pleasure?

[1]Studdert Kennedy, *The Wicket Gate* (London: Hodder & Stoughton, 1923), pp41–42.

7.   What is God Looking For?

[1]Studdert Kennedy, *The Wicket Gate*, pp138–139.

8.   What if I'm Not Good Enough?

[1]Geoffrey Anketell Studdert Kennedy, *Food for the Fed Up* (Hodder & Stoughton, 1921), pp65–67.

[2]Studdert Kennedy, *The Wicket Gate*, pp61-62.

[3]Studdert Kennedy, *The Unutterable Beauty*, p104.

9. What is the World All About?

[1]Studdert Kennedy, *The Word and the Work* (London: Longmans, 1926), pp1-2,18-19.

[2]Studdert Kennedy, *The Hardest Part*, pp116-117.

10. What is the Church Doing Here?

[1]Studdert Kennedy, *Rough Talks by a Padre*, pp17-18,20-22.

[2]Studdert Kennedy, *The Wicket Gate*, p79.

[3]Studdert Kennedy, *The Unutterable Beauty*, p40.

11. What is the Power of Prayer?

[1]Studdert Kennedy, *The Hardest Part*, pp101-119.

[2]*Ibid*, p119.

[3]*Ibid*, pp113-114.

[4]*Ibid*, p110.

[5]*Ibid*, p111.

12. What Can We Do About Suffering?

[1]Studdert Kennedy, *The Word and the Work*, pp57-60.

[2]*Ibid*, pp3-4.

13. What Should I Do With My Money?

[1]Studdert Kennedy, *The Wicket Gate*, pp121-123.

14. What is the Secret of Good Sex and Love?

[1]Studdert Kennedy, *Rough Talks by a Padre*, pp106-111.

[2]*Ibid*, p109.

[3]*Ibid*, p117.

[4]Studdert Kennedy, *The Warrior, the Woman and the Christ*, p58.

[5]Geoffrey Anketell Studdert Kennedy, *I Pronounce Them* (New York: George H. Doran, 1927) pp7-8.

[6]Studdert Kennedy, *Rough Talks by a Padre*, p115.

15. What is the Point of Work?

[1]Studdert Kennedy, *The Unutterable Beauty*, pp98-99.

[2]Studdert Kennedy, *Democracy and the Dog Collar* (London: Hodder & Stoughton, 1921), pp99-100.

[3]Studdert Kennedy, *The Wicket Gate*, pp76-79.

[4]Studdert Kennedy, *The Hardest Part*, p7.

[5]Studdert Kennedy, *The Wicket Gate*, pp36,40.

[6]Studdert Kennedy, *The Word and the Work*, pp75-76

[7]Studdert Kennedy, *The Unutterable Beauty*, p111.

FAITH ON THE FRONTLINE

In *Faith on the Frontline*, serving and
ex members of the military, as well as
their families, tell us how their faith
has helped them face pressure. Their
honest accounts help us explore how
our faith can stand up to life's daily
battles on the spiritual front line.

ISBN: 978-1-78259-261-7

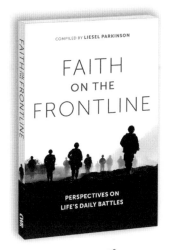

COFFEE WITH GOD

Coffee with God is a unique collection of reflection on the Psalms
written by women with a military connection. The writers weave into
each day, issues faced acutely by those connected with the Military,
such as deployment, the loneliness of those left at home, the upheaval
of moving and the camaraderie of living with others.

ISBN: 978-1-85345-841-5

For current prices visit **www.cwr.org.uk/store**
Available online or from Christian bookshops

Courses and seminars

Publishing and media

Conference facilities

Transforming lives

CWR's vision is to enable people to experience personal transformation through applying God's Word to their lives and relationships.

Our Bible-based training and resources help people around the world to:
• Grow in their walk with God
• Understand and apply Scripture to their lives
• Resource themselves and their church
• Develop pastoral care and counselling skills
• Train for leadership
• Strengthen relationships, marriage and family life and much more.

Our insightful writers provide daily Bible-reading notes and other resources for all ages, and our experienced course designers and presenters have gained an international reputation for excellence and effectiveness.

CWR's Training and Conference Centres in Surrey and East Sussex, England, provide excellent facilities in idyllic settings – ideal for both learning and spiritual refreshment.

CWR Applying God's Word
to everyday life and relationships

CWR, Waverley Abbey House,
Waverley Lane, Farnham,
Surrey GU9 8EP, UK

Telephone: **+44 (0)1252 784700**
Email: **info@cwr.org.uk**
Website: **www.cwr.org.uk**

Registered Charity No 294387
Company Registration No 1990308